COURAGE UNDER FIRE

YILDA B. RIVERA

Courage Under Fire
By Yilda Rivera

ISBN-10 0983100977
ISBN-13 97809831009-7-3

Library of Congress Control Number: 2014906886

All material is the original work of Yilda Rivera copyright © 2014, all rights reserved. Material may not be published, reproduced, distributed, transmitted, displayed, or used in any form or by any means. For specific permission of use, contact the publisher for written permission.

THE HOLY BIBLE, NEW INTERNATIONAL VERSION®, NIV®
Copyright © 1973, 1978, 1984, 2011 by Biblica, Inc.® Used by permission.
All rights reserved worldwide.

Scripture taken from the New King James Version®. Copyright © 1982 by Thomas Nelson, Inc. Used by permission. All rights reserved.

Scripture taken from the New Century Version®. Copyright © 2005 by Thomas Nelson, Inc. Used by permission. All rights reserved.

The ESV® Bible (The Holy Bible, English Standard Version®) copyright © 2001 by Crossway, a publishing ministry of Good News Publishers. ESV® Text Edition: 2011. The ESV® text has been reproduced in cooperation with and by permission of Good News Publishers. All rights reserved.

Scripture quotations marked (NLT) are taken from the Holy Bible, New Living Translation, copyright © 1996, 2004, 2007 by Tyndale House Foundation. Used by permission of Tyndale House Publishers, Inc., Carol Stream, Illinois 60188. All rights reserved.

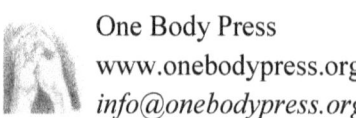
One Body Press
www.onebodypress.org
info@onebodypress.org

Table of Contents

TABLE OF CONTENTS	III
DEDICATION	V
ACKNOWLEDGEMENTS	VI
PREFACE	VII
INTRODUCTION	VIII

THE DIAGNOSIS 1

A PREMONITION?	3
A ROUTINE MAMMOGRAM	7
THE BIOPSY	11
THE DAY	13

SHARING THE NEWS 21

SHARING THE NEWS WITH FRIENDS AND FAMILY	23
SHARING THE NEWS WITH KIDS	29

THE QUESTIONS 33

THE CROSSROAD	35
WHEN GOD SPEAKS	45

THE TREATMENT 49

ON THE VERGE OF A MIRACLE	51
THE SURGERIES	57
CARPE DIEM	65
CHEMO STARTS	69
COPING WITH FRUSTRATION	77
COPING WITH HAIR LOSS	81
A SOURCE OF INSPIRATION	93
COPING WITH NEUTROPENIA	103
COPING WITH EXHAUSTION	113
COPING WITH UNCERTAINTY	119
COPING WITH ANXIETY	129
COPING WITH APPEARANCE	135
COPING WITH RADIATION	141
ONE MORE DAY TO BE THANKFUL	147
COPING WITH THE "LEFTOVERS"	149

THE AFTERMATH 155
- DEALING WITH THE AFTERMATH 157
- A NEW SONG 169

THE TESTIMONY 171
- HOPE AND JOY IN THE DARK 173
- A NEW STANCE 175
- THE FIVE W'S 181
- THE PRAYERS 183
- THE SWORD 187

NOTES 199

Dedication

To my husband, Angel – Thanks for your love. It is a joy to love God with you by my side. Thank you for being such a wonderful father for our boys, an amazing husband, my love and my best friend. Thank you for all your sacrifice, patience and support during this journey. I love you.

To my sons, Alejandro and Angel Gabriel – You have inspired me and continue to inspire me. You are two wonderful blessings in my life. I love you. Always remember how special you are and that nothing in all creation will be able to separate you from the love of God. May the fullness of God who fills everything in every way give you the Spirit of wisdom and revelation so that you may know Him better, and that your heart may be enlightened in order that you may know the hope to which He has called you. Do not ever forget the child in you.

To my parents, Santiago and Doris – Thanks for all the sacrifices you made for me; for those that I'm aware of and for the ones I am not even aware of. I wouldn't be the person I am today if it were not for the seed of faith that you planted in me. Thank you for all your support over the years. I will always be grateful to you. I love you.

Acknowledgements

Thank you God because you never let go of me.

Thank you Todd for helping me to get my story out to the world. Thank you for believing in me, sometimes more than myself. It's a joy to call you my friend and my brother in Christ.

Blanca, thank you for that wonderful memory of full happiness—the moment I saw that yellow cab approaching home knowing that you were there. I still have that vivid memory in my mind. Thank you for the sacrifice you made in taking time away from your children to be with me a few days. Thanks to them and to Juan Carlos for letting me borrow "Mom."

Thank you Madelyn for your visit, it inspired me. Thank you for that beautiful prayer you elevated for each of us that day. It truly touched our hearts.

Finally, thank you so much to the many friends and family who were always encouraging and inspiring me to keep on fighting. It was such a great feeling of joy to find your notes of support or letters along the way.

Preface

I hope that anybody facing any struggle or questions about life can find courage and inspiration throughout this book. I started writing this book based on my journey through cancer while I was still a cancer patient, but later I realized that my story goes beyond my cancer battle. It was a battle against uncertainty, fear, doubts and lies of hopelessness. This book is not only about cancer . . . it's about fight, hope, courage and faith.

I share with you my lifeline during this cancer battle and battle of faith. I share as well many smiles and laughs along the journey. Yes, I refused to let the cancer take that away from me . . . the ability to laugh.

This book is also addressed to those warriors who are fighting or have fought cancer, to those persons who know a warrior and to those who want to be aware of the warriors who are out there and want to understand a little of what the battle is like.

For those of you battling cancer, it's an honor to write for you. It's an honor to relate to you. I hope that by reading this book you find a source or courage and strength in your journey. I hope that the many experiences I share about my journey give you hope and the main understanding that you are not alone. I hope you get the understanding that it is okay to have mixed emotions and that you can find courage and your way one step at a time, one breath at a time.

For those of you who know someone battling with cancer, I hope this book gives you some understanding about the fight that the warrior you know may be going through, and the knowledge and tools to stand by their side to go through the fight with them. I hope it will help you to listen to them and be a warrior yourself with them.

For those who know a cancer survivor or those who are survivors, I hope you find in this book inspiration and the knowledge to share with others what the cancer cannot take from us . . . hope—the hope and the determination to cherish every moment that we are given. Keep up the good fight!

Introduction

Many think that the battle with cancer starts the moment that you begin your cancer treatment and ends the moment you finish your treatment. The truth is that the battle starts at the moment you know you have been diagnosed with cancer and continues even further by dealing with the "leftovers" of what the treatment caused and facing life itself with courage. It is not just a battle of overcoming the harshness of the treatment—in my case breast cancer treatment—but a battle of faith. Whatever hardship you may face, faith is what is going to get you overcome the odds.

Not only you will be battling with all the direct and associated effects of the treatment, whatever it may be (chemotherapy, surgery, radiation, medication, a combination of these), but you; will find yourself battling as well against fear, doubt, isolation, anger, guilt, confusion, anguish and maybe depression and hopelessness. Your health care team can be helping you to physically recover and endure against the physical effects of the treatment and maybe to deal with the emotional impacts associated with it. However, you are the one who has to be determined to fight the battle of faith. You will discover that despite uncertainty and chaos, there are still choices we could make.

Faith is what is going to keep you afloat no matter what your circumstances may be. Your love ones will have questions as well and will have their own battle with fear, doubt, anger, guilt and even depression. That is why faith is what is going to get you through; whether you are the one with cancer or a friend/family of someone with cancer. Faith will bring you harmony.

As of me, in my battle with breast cancer, faith was my shield and the Word of God my sword. Prayer was my food, my lifeline.

> *But he said to me, "My grace is sufficient for you, for my power is made perfect in weakness." Therefore I will boast more gladly about my weaknesses, so that Christ's power may rest on me.*
> *(2 Corinthians 12:9, NIV)*

These words were key to finding strength, hope and inspiration in my fight with breast cancer. "It is not about what I know, or what I see, but *who* I know." I kept repeating that to myself.

> *So do not fear, for I am with you;*
> *do not be dismayed, for I am your God.*
> *I will strengthen you and help you;*
> *I will uphold you with my righteous right hand.*
> *(Isaiah 41:10, NIV)*

The cancer warrior will be faced with many questions and decisions for which there are no definitive answers. Cancer treatment is a work in progress. There have been many advances, but there are still many unknowns. There are no guarantees.

During my battle with uncertainty I leaned on God. Faith helped me to see beyond my circumstances. At some point I had to let go holding on to my children and my husband to free myself from the fear of loss and to avoid the frustration of not having control of the situation. So I chose instead to see them as blessings granted by God. Meditating in those blessings helped me to smile by remembering many moments of our lives together that I had recorded in a journal many years before. Through that, I discovered a courage inside, a power beyond my understanding that kept me going, a fire that gave me the strength to battle pain, fear, doubt, isolation, anger, guilt, confusion, anguish and hopelessness. Those short and simple journal entries and memories that helped me feel joy and fed me during the battle with cancer are presented as separate blocks called "*Remembering.*" Thoughts I had while in the journey through breast cancer, I present as "*Journal Entry.*"

In the last chapter, I have collected some of the many Bible verses that spoke to me in different situations. The various Bible versions and the numbers indicating notes and references are grouped per chapter at the end of the book.

When I think about my journey through cancer, I realize that I was each day on the verge of a miracle. God was transforming all my fears and the chaos around and inside me into peace. He was transforming my darkness into light. He was filling my loneliness with his presence. My pain and grief, He was transforming those into joy. In my nakedness and vulnerability, He was clothing me with His love. I was seeing His hand on me. He was making me able to walk through the waters. I was experiencing the direct intervention of the power of God in my life, to me that was a miracle—a miracle occurring day after day after day.

THE DIAGNOSIS

A Premonition?

I posted the following passage on the "Onebodyministries.org" blog before being diagnosed with breast cancer. I will let you read it and judge for yourself if it was a premonition of what was to come the next month. To me, God was preparing my heart for the road ahead. He was guarding me and reassuring me of His presence and light even before I was aware of what was going on inside me.

January 20, 2011:

I'll Be with You

My Lord, if I ever doubt or question myself if I can do what you want me to do, may I always remember your Word of trust:

But Moses said to God, "Who am I that I should go to Pharaoh and bring the Israelites out of Egypt" And God said, "I will be with you." (Exodus 3:11-12, NIV)

In the New King James Version, the word "certainly" accompanies God's reply to Moses: "I will certainly be with you." This way the Lord's pledge to accompany you along the walk, to be with you and in you, is your certainty of the words expressed in Psalms 121, NIV:

*^{1}I lift up my eyes to the mountains—
where does my help come from?
^{2}My help comes from the LORD,
the Maker of heaven and earth.
^{3}He will not let your foot slip—
he who watches over you will not slumber;
^{4}indeed, he who watches over Israel
will neither slumber nor sleep.
^{5}The LORD watches over you—
the LORD is your shade at your right hand;
^{6}the sun will not harm you by day,
nor the moon by night.
^{7}The LORD will keep you from all harm—
he will watch over your life;
^{8}the LORD will watch over your coming and going
both now and forevermore.*

A Premonition?

It is amazing how His Word speaks to us. How it guides us in every step through the Holy Spirit. What is our call then? Our call is to seek Him, to know Him more, to trust Him. It is a matter of will . . . a matter of voluntarily choosing to love Him and letting Him guide us through the many mysteries or challenges we could face. When we trust the One who gave himself for us, in every aspect of our lives, we start living a purpose driven life. Things start falling into place, we know our goal even though we might not see the end of the way, and the mystery described in Ephesians 1:3-10 and also mentioned in Colossians 1:26-27 starts to be revealed in our lives in every step of the way. It is a matter of "emptying" ourselves with things that tie us or entangle us, in order to be filled by God's grace and *"the fullness of him who fills everything in every way"* (Ephesians 1:23, NIV).

So, if it is a matter of lack of trust, do not be discouraged . . . just be honest and pray in His will, and be prepared to receive God's grace (you are invited to read the rest of the passage below to see what happened after verse 24):

*"If you can?" said Jesus. "Everything is possible
for one who believes."
Immediately the boy's father exclaimed,
"I do believe; help me overcome my unbelief!"
(Mark 9:23-24, NIV)*

Is it a lack of courage or strength? He will provide. Let the Lord guide you:

*Your word is a lamp for my feet, and a light on my path.
(Psalms 119:105, NIV)*

Surrender your love and your trust to the One who loves you dearly. Seek Him and grow in his knowledge and in prayer. And may "the fullness of him who fills everything in every way," as per Ephesians 1, "give you the Spirit of wisdom and revelation, so that you may know him better" and "that the eyes of your heart may be enlightened in order that you may know the hope to which he has called you." In Jesus name, amen.

Every time I read this, I know that the Lord was preparing myself for the road ahead. He was reminding me about the tools I was going to need—will, willingness and faith. The part about voluntarily choosing Him to guide us and trust Him was true every day during my breast cancer journey and is true to this day. There were so many things going on inside me and on the outside—many beyond my control. However, one thing I could control was to pray and commit myself every day to trust God so He could guide me. He helped me through the journey and He was with me every step, sometimes even carrying me in His own arms.

A Routine Mammogram

In my thirty-nine years old I was probably in better shape and health than when I was in my 20s—or so I thought. I was playing soccer. I could play one-hour games straight without substitution. I was taking tennis lessons and I loved the intensity, the fast pace and dynamics of the game. I was doing martial arts with my kids. I was feeling stronger than ever. I was eating fairly healthy and had my personal goals to increase my intake of fruits, fluids and vegetables even more. I was ready to face my 40s in strength and was getting ready with optimism for the transformative years to come.

When I turned 40, I scheduled the routine medical exams, adding a mammogram to the list of standard procedures. My blood pressure was excellent, my weight was good, nothing worthy of concern. However, one thing merited a phone call from my gynecologist one day. There was some concern about the results of my mammogram that required a second test.

The doctor's office scheduled the appointment for me to make sure the radiologist could be there to read the results that same day. The gynecologist explained me that although the mammogram didn't show any calcifications[1], which would be an item of concern, it was routine to request another reading if there was something that the radiologist wanted to get a better look at.

I thought that the reason for the second reading was that I had fibrocystic breasts[2]. When I was in college I had had an ultrasound test done that confirmed a normal nodule and breast changes due to that condition.

The date came to have the second mammogram done. I was told that the radiologist wanted to repeat tests on both breasts. Remembering how uncomfortable a mammogram is, I sighed, put the gown on, and mentally prepared myself. Once the second mammogram was completed, the technologist told me to wait and not to change clothes until the radiologist read the results. They wanted me to wait. So I waited.

After a short time another woman I hadn't met approached me in the patient waiting area.

"Are you Mrs. Rivera?" the lady asked me.

"Yes."

A Routine Mammogram

"Mrs. Rivera, the doctor is recommending to conduct an ultrasound on the left breast."

"Oh! Okay . . . When should I be scheduling the—"

"Oh, not at all! The doctor wants us to do the ultrasound right now," said the woman. "She wants to be here to read the results immediately because there are some areas shown in the left breast mammogram she wants to verify. Is that okay with you?"

"Yes. Okay . . . Perfect. I—I'm already here . . . Why not? Thank you," I stuttered.

"Please come with me to show you to your room."

The urgency of the radiology doctor built up some anxiety within me. I stayed there in the ultrasound room. I was looking through the window blinds, looking at the ceiling; I guess I was trying to avoid thinking about the situation. I put some music in my phone to avoid listening to my thoughts. Then I remained calm while waiting for the ultrasound technologist to start.

My cell phone rang. I saw the screen and it was my husband. For sure he wanted to know how everything went. I didn't want to pick it up. I didn't want to worry him. After all, I wouldn't know what to tell him. I finally decided to answer it.

"I'm still here in the clinic . . . call you back later," I told him in a whispering voice.

"Oh, Okay!" Angel began to say, "I only wanted to know how you are doing."

Then I heard two gentle knocks on the door. The door opened and the ultrasound technologist came into the room.

"I gotta go. I'll call you back. Love you," I said to Angel softly over the phone.

"Okay. Love you too. Bye."

The technologist started explaining me what she was going to do with the ultrasound and the reason the doctor wanted to do it right away. She told me the radiologist had seen something of concern that she wanted to get a better look at with an ultrasound. She asked me to wait there in the ultrasound room once the procedure was complete in case the radiologist wanted to discuss anything with me. In my mind, I was pleased by the concern the doctor was showing to me, but at the same time, I couldn't stop the feeling that something was going on . . . something not good.

My heart was beating rapidly. I was repeating in my mind Psalm 42:5 (NIV): *"Why, my soul, are you downcast? Why so disturbed within me? Put your hope in God, for I will yet praise him, my Savior and my God."* So I started praising God in my heart and acknowledging that He was bigger than whatever situation I was in.

I was watching the lady performing the procedure when suddenly she started concentrating on one particular area and taking measurements with the hand scanner. She went back and forth around my left breast and stopped again in that same area while looking at the screen. She made some notes, but I couldn't see what she was writing. She tried to show me what she was looking at and why, but looking at the screen didn't make any difference, I only saw shadows. I mentioned my fibrocystic breasts and she said something about comparing the normal nodules and breast changes with the surrounding tissue. She told me to wait in the room while the radiologist checked the results. I don't recall how long I waited, but it was not long before I heard a knock on the door and a woman entered the room.

She introduced herself as the radiologist and thanked me for being so patient. I thanked her in return for her attention and concern. She told me that she wanted to take a closer look at one area. She put some more ultrasound gel on my already "beaten" breast and began her examination. She explained why she was concerned about a suspicious area. She told me that even though they didn't find calcifications—I recalled that my gynecologist had used that same word—they could recommend a biopsy if they found a suspicious tissue. Abruptly she stopped moving the hand scanner. She had found the spot. She became silent as she moved the scanner slowly and pressed it firmly against my breast. She asked me to move toward my side. In total silence she concentrated in the monitor. Suddenly I heard her make a sound that led me to believe she found what she was looking for. She pressed the scanner harder and barely moved it. I waited. Then, I thought I heard the word "calcifications" spoken under her breath, probably for herself. My heart jumped and kept pounding inside me. She stopped what she was doing and while I cleaned off the gel she kindly and firmly told me that she was definitely going to recommend a biopsy for the left breast.

There were so many things on my mind that it was difficult to process all the information. Remembering that I had told Angel that I would call, I walked slowly out of the clinic, sat on a bench and called him. To avoid worrying him, I told him that the radiologist would keep looking at the results and might recommend a biopsy. To try to keep him calm I told him about the normal nodule I once had and about my fibrocystic breasts[2]. I quickly changed the subject and we talked about other things.

My gynecologist called that very afternoon. I was already back in my office. He asked me what the radiologist told me and he said that that was exactly what he was recommending, a biopsy. He described me what the biopsy procedure would be like, asked me what I wanted to do and asked if I had any questions. Without hesitation I responded that I was going to go through with the procedure.

Surprisingly, I didn't feel any fear. I was feeling a strange and overpowering sense of purpose to get my concerns out of the way. I leaned back on my chair and reached for the copy of the New Testament that I always kept at my desk, which also has the books of Proverbs and Psalms. I said to myself, "Lord I know you are here with me."

I sighed. I opened the pocket New Testament and read Psalm 119:105 (NIV): *"Your word is a lamp to my feet and a light to my path."* I prayed, "God you will give me courage, you will show me the way."

The Biopsy

Angel went with me to the biopsy. We arrived early. The nurse escorted me into the preparation room to help me with the paperwork and explain the details of the procedure. "The mass, the tissue, the lump . . ." Those words kept echoing in my mind. "Geez; I have a mass, some strange tissue inside."

The more I repeated that, the more I realized that I had a suspicious tissue in my body that was of concern to doctors, something not normal that needed to be sampled. While they were preparing me for the procedure, this verse of Psalm 42:5 (NIV) came to my mind:

> *Why, my soul, are you downcast?*
> *Why so disturbed within me?*
> *Put your hope in God, for I will yet praise him,*
> *my Savior and my God.*

Also in my heart were the opening verses of Psalms 121, NIV:

> *I lift up my eyes to the mountains—*
> *where does my help come from?*
> *My help comes from the LORD,*
> *the Maker of heaven and earth.*

The biopsy started. The position I had to maintain during the procedure and the procedure itself were a little uncomfortable. There was the doctor with a long instrument to take the sample, the technologist with the ultrasound scanner and a nurse who kept me calm and comfortable. They were all very considerate. They explained everything they were doing. They gave me a pillow, a cushion to keep my position on my side, and another cushion to support my legs. They were making sure to take care of me and not solely worry about the procedure.

The biopsy took longer than expected. The stubborn mass didn't want to cooperate. It was thick, it was hard and it moved every time the doctor tried to get a sample with the needle. The situation was frustrating and exhausting. The nurse and the doctor did an excellent job keeping me calm. Finally, they were able to take enough samples and put an X-ray marker in the area so they could easily locate it again when necessary. They told me they would send the results to my doctor and that I would be contacted in about 5 days.

The Biopsy

I tried not to think about the biopsy in the following days. I was determined to put my anxiety behind me. I didn't want to alarm my parents so I didn't talk about the biopsy when we spoke over the phone. Even Angel and I didn't speak about it.

I found myself many times thinking about the fact that we had just left Puerto Rico less than a year ago to move to Texas. We left family and friends behind. I became very nostalgic during those days after the biopsy.

During those days I had in my mind a song that I used to hear often in Puerto Rico by the group "Tercer Cielo." The song was titled "Creeré" ("I Will Believe"). The lyrics assert that even if the wind blows on your face, you shouldn't stop believing; that if God is at your side you will have everything necessary to rise up and have strength. I was also thinking that *"all things God works for the good of those who love him, who have been called according to his purpose"* (Romans 8:28, NIV).

Other Bible verses that gave me comfort during those days while I awaited the biopsy results were Psalm 42:8 and Peter 5:7. Many times I didn't know what to pray for or didn't know how to put my thoughts into words. I held the Bible many times against my heart and asked the Lord to speak to me. I needed to hear His voice and feel His presence. I wanted to see beyond my circumstances. Occasionally I was praying and ran out of words. I just stood there still in His presence and I didn't want to go away from it. I was at a loss for words, not knowing what to ask or say . But I knew that it was okay; it didn't matter. His peace was surrounding me.

Yet the Lord will command His lovingkindness in the daytime,
and in the night His song shall be with me and my prayer
unto the God of my life.
(Psalms 42:8, KJV)

Cast all your anxiety on him because he cares for you.
(1 Peter 5:7, NIV)

The Day

Three days had passed since the biopsy. I was in my office that afternoon working on the computer, keeping my mind busy. My cell phone rang; it was a call from the doctor's office. My heart jumped and my hands were trembling.

"Hello?"

"Am I speaking with Mrs. Yilda Rivera?" it was my gynecologist's voice. He sounded friendly.

"Hi, Dr. Calderón!" I replied trying to mask the nervousness in my voice.

"Yilda . . . Mrs. Yilda I need to see you," he said softly and caringly.

My heart started beating faster; and after a long sigh, I couldn't hide my concern any longer and replied:

"Yes doctor?"

"Yilda, Yilda . . ." his voice was deep, "is it possible for me to see you today?"

"Oh! Okay! Certainly . . . Hmm—"

"I know we don't have a scheduled appointment, so if you can come today, just say your name to the receptionist and tell her I called you in."

My heart continued pounding hard in my chest and every beat deafened my thoughts. With a deep breath, I continued:

"Okay Dr. Calderón. I'll be there," my voice was firm now. "Can you give me any news now?" I asked knowing that it wouldn't feel good what I was about to hear, but both of us knew what we were talking about.

"The biopsy results came in," he was trying to prepare me with every word. "I don't like them . . . the pathology came positive."

Those words went right through my stomach like an arrow.

"Oh no!" I replied smoothly after taking a deep breath, "I'll be there. I—I'll see you in a while."

The Day

I hung up the phone. Time seemed to stop. I suddenly felt as if I were inside a bubble, suspended in time. My pulse was loud in my head, inside my ears. My feet and hands felt frozen. I felt a chilling sensation from the very core of me. A huge black hole was originating in the center of my stomach and was sucking me in. Thank God I was sitting, because I lost all feeling in my legs. After a few moments, I stretched and moved my legs slowly to make sure they were still working.

The stubborn mass finally had a name, cancer . . . breast cancer. Wow! I remained seated with my elbows on my desk and my hands on my face. Sometimes I remained still and sometimes I swung back and forth in my chair. I took several deep breaths—each of them so hard to take. I wiped off some tears and looked around me. I was feeling every beat of my heart. That was the only thing I could hear at that moment. I was trying hard to hold myself together.

I heard conversation in the corridor. I tried to estimate how many people were around the office. I had to be able to stand up to make it through the corridor, to the main hallway, and then continue walking to the nearest restroom to find some space away from everything. I took a deep breath and stood up.

> *Why, my soul, are you downcast?*
> *Why so disturbed within me?*
> *Put your hope in God,*
> *for I will yet praise him,*
> *my Savior and my God.*
> *(Psalms 42:5, NIV)*

While walking, I prayed. "Oh God, I know you are here with me. You know how I'm feeling right now. You have a purpose in all this. I cannot see it. I cannot understand it. But I know you are here. Show me the way. May you be my strength."

I started walking slowly through the office, hoping that nobody would stop me or speak to me. I didn't know if I was able to hide my expression.

I successfully made it to the restroom without being stopped or spoken to. I splashed some cold water on my face. I thought about Abraham when he was going up the hill to sacrifice his own son . . . not knowing or understanding the difficult task ahead. Every step must have been unbearable, but he found strength to keep walking ahead with the certainty that God was going to provide.

> *So Abraham called that place The Lord Will Provide. And to this day it is said, "On the mountain of the Lord it will be provided."*
> *(Genesis 22:14, NIV)*

Then I prayed to my Lord from the depths of my soul:

"Oh, God. I'm going to walk this path. Although I feel troubled—I cannot hide it from you—I know that you are here, and that you are going to be with me. Your eye is upon me. I shall go and praise you. Please hold me and help me walk every step. May your great name be glorified in me. May your glory shine on me."

Walking back to my desk I felt as if I were moving in slow motion. I needed to call Angel to ask him to pick up the kids at school since I was going to the doctor's office right after work. I prepared myself to talk to him. After a few minutes, I gathered the courage to call him.

"Hello precious!" I whispered.

"Hi sweetie. What's up?" he said cheerfully.

"Could you pick up the kids at school today? I'll be home late."

"Yes, no problem. Got a lot of work today?"

"I'm going to the see the doctor. He called me . . . It's not good."

"Oh no!" he sighed in unpleasant surprise. He paused and then he added, "Ma . . . I love you." he said softly. His voice changed.

"Thank you, Pa. Love you too."

"God is with us," he added.

"Yes I know. I've been repeating that to myself. I know He has something for us in all this."

"God will provide," he was sad but firm in what he was saying. He sucked in a deep breath, and let it all come out slowly. "I'm here . . . you know that."

The Day

"Don't tell anyone yet, please. Let me digest this first," I said softly between silent tears.

"Please drive carefully," he was concerned.

"Don't worry Papa. I'm calm. I'm strangely calm. God is filling me with the peace that goes beyond all understanding . . ." I paused for a moment, "we'll talk later, Okay?"

"Okay."

After I hung up I was left alone with only my thoughts. At the end of the day I left the office and walked to my car. I started it and turned off the radio as if trying to silence my thoughts. I couldn't control the tears that soon began to flow down my cheeks again. The drive to the doctor's office turned into a conversation with God. I was pouring my whole self to Him, reaching and holding His hand. He was a rock in the middle of the storm. I could visualize Matthew 14:22-31 in which Jesus appears walking on the water toward his disciples who were in a small boat tossed about by a strong wind and heavy waves:

> [22] *Immediately Jesus made the disciples get into the boat and go on ahead of him to the other side, while he dismissed the crowd. . . .* [24] *and the boat was already a considerable distance from land, buffeted by the waves because the wind was against it.*
> [25] *Shortly before dawn Jesus went out to them, walking on the lake.* [26] *When the disciples saw him walking on the lake, they were terrified. "It's a ghost," they said, and cried out in fear.*
> [27] *But Jesus immediately said to them: "Take courage! It is I. Don't be afraid."*
> [28] *"Lord, if it's you," Peter replied, "tell me to come to you on the water."*
> [29] *"Come," he said.*
> *Then Peter got down out of the boat, walked on the water and came toward Jesus.* [30] *But when he saw the wind, he was afraid and, beginning to sink, cried out, "Lord, save me!"*
> [31] *Immediately Jesus reached out his hand and caught him. "You of little faith," he said, "why did you doubt?"*

Therefore, I was certain that the more the storm intensified and roared at me, the more I knew my Father was with me and held me. I had an image in my mind of Peter walking on the water in the middle of the wind and strong waves, walking against all odds. I knew that if I started fearing and paying attention to the uncertainty and harsh wind around me I would sink, so I was determined to have my sight firmly on my Lord and my faith with the One who's calling me.

I knew that if I started fearing and paying attention to the uncertainty and harsh wind around me I would sink, so I was determined to have my sight firmly on my Lord and my faith with the One who's calling me.

"Oh Lord. You will provide. Thank you because you are about to show me your grace. Prepare my heart. Take care of my family. Take care of my kids. They are yours. Hold me in this path."

My blog posting in "onebodyministries.org" on March 29, 2011, on "The Day" is next:

No Matter How Your Circumstances May Be

Psalm 42, NIV:

> [1] As the deer pants for streams of water,
> so my soul pants for you, my God.
> [2] My soul thirsts for God, for the living God.
> When can I go and meet with God?
> [3] My tears have been my food
> day and night,
> while men say to me all day long,
> "Where is your God?"
> [4] These things I remember
> as I pour out my soul:
> how I used to go to the house of God,
> under the protection of the Mighty One
> with shouts of joy and praise
> among the festive throng.

The Day

⁵ Why, my soul, are you downcast?
   Why so disturbed within me?
   Put your hope in God,
     for I will yet praise him,
     my Savior and my God.
⁶ My soul is downcast within me;
   therefore I will remember you
   from the land of the Jordan,
the heights of Hermon—from Mount Mizar.
⁷ Deep calls to deep
   in the roar of your waterfalls;
   all your waves and breakers
     have swept over me.
⁸ By day the LORD directs his love,
   at night his song is with me—
   a prayer to the God of my life.
⁹ I say to God my Rock,
   "Why have you forgotten me?
   Why must I go about mourning,
     oppressed by the enemy?"
¹⁰ My bones suffer mortal agony
     as my foes taunt me,
   saying to me all day long,
     "Where is your God?"
¹¹ Why, my soul, are you downcast?
   Why so disturbed within me?
   Put your hope in God,
     for I will yet praise him,
     my Savior and my God.

What this Psalm says to me is that no matter how difficult your circumstances may be, no matter how disturbed is your soul or how your ground is being shaken, put your hope in the Lord. Rest in his promises, take heart and wait for his moment, for his refreshing rain to be poured upon you.

I put my prayers before you, oh Lord of my life.

COURAGE UNDER FIRE

[7] Hear my voice when I call, LORD;
be merciful to me and answer me.
[8] My heart says of you, "Seek his face!"
Your face, LORD, I will seek. . . .
[13] I remain confident of this:
I will see the goodness of the LORD
in the land of the living.
[14] Wait for the LORD;
be strong and take heart
and wait for the LORD.
(Psalms 27:7-8,13-14, NIV)

SHARING THE NEWS

Sharing the News with Friends and Family

I shared the news that I had had a biopsy and was awaiting for the results with no one but my husband and Todd, a friend from work. As a result, my diagnosis was going to be an unexpected and unpleasant surprise for nearly all of my friends and family.

I knew that at some point I had to reveal the results to Todd. He was praying for me and he knew that my results would be back soon. I knew that at some point I had to tell my parents who were an ocean away from me. I couldn't ask my husband to keep this as a secret to himself indefinitely because just as I needed to confide in him to be strong I knew he would need to confide this to his family as well. This was such a very heavy load that I knew it was not going to be healthy to hide it.

The key question was, "How am I going to tell my family and friends about this?" It was too difficult already to hear myself saying, "I have breast cancer." I didn't want to worry anybody. Maybe I didn't have to tell anybody until after the surgery and tell them, "It's already taken care of." But would that be really true? There were too many questions ahead. There were still more exams to be done for cancer staging[1] and many decisions to be made when I didn't even knew the right questions to ask. I hadn't even have selected an oncologist or a surgeon.

Starting One-by-One

I couldn't hide this from my close friends. Friends who even though we were separated by miles and miles, were very close to my heart.

I thought about my mom and how she would react to the news. I got worried that she would worry too much. I only had the first biopsy that confirmed breast cancer (Invasive Ductal Carcinoma) and I still didn't know the stage of it or how aggressive it was. I decided not to call her until I had more information.

First I decided to call a very dear childhood friend of mine, Blanca. I had to vent outside of my immediate family circle. Angel was with the kids. I told Angel not to say anything to the kids until I was ready to tell them. I went outside to the backyard and sat on the deck for a while. I felt the breeze and

Sharing the News With Friends and Family

started praying. While praying, I thanked the Lord for His presence. My prayer was like a quiet conversation with God. I asked God to prepare my friend's heart for what I was about to tell her. When I felt at peace, I called my friend.

To my surprise, Blanca was just getting over laryngitis. I still have no idea how she got the strength to speak so gracefully to me. We talked about how the Lord would show His magnificent glory in this situation. She told me beautiful things. God was using her to raise my confidence and strength. During the conversation I shed slow tears and sometimes laughed. I requested her continuous prayers. We sent each other strong and big hugs. I felt relieved.

I remained alone for a while, listening to the birds in the trees and feeling the quiet breeze on my face. I meditated on Jesus' words on Mathew 6:26, NKJV:

> *Look at the birds of the air, for they neither sow*
> *nor reap nor gather into barns;*
> *yet your heavenly Father feeds them.*
> *Are you not of more value than they?*

I meditated on how Abraham felt in Genesis 22 when he was going up the high mountain with the difficult task of sacrificing his own son Isaac. He had such a difficult task ahead and in the midst of uncertainty, he remained faithful. I imagined how troubled he must have felt and how he chose to trust God regardless. I pictured him in my mind repeating to himself, "God will provide." Therefore, I constantly repeated, "God will provide" to myself. It didn't matter if I didn't understand my situation, the truth was that God was going to provide.

Maybe God wants to show me something that otherwise I wouldn't be able to see. God will provide...

"I am willing to go up this steep hill to face this difficult task ahead in faith. Maybe God wants to show me something that otherwise I wouldn't be able to see. God will provide and He will be of provision on His time."

COURAGE UNDER FIRE

With this in mind I called my friend Todd, who was waiting for my call, and told him. He was praying for me as he knew I had a biopsy done and I was awaiting the results. He was very sad to hear the news, but at the same time I knew his prayers were going to be with me as well.

"Praying" the News

I realized that when I prayed before telling someone the breast cancer news, I was more calm. Later that night, I decided to reveal the news to a few persons at a time. First I selected three friends. I sat at my computer and wrote an e-mail message that would help me talk to them later on.

These were the words I chose:

> Hello friends,
>
> I'm writing you so that you keep me in your prayers. There is no way to decorate what I'm going to say . . . so I'm going straight to the point. Today I received the news that a biopsy I had on a nodule in the breast came out positive. So far, the next step will be to visit an Oncologist and a Surgeon to explore the alternatives. Thus, with honor, I'm joining the frontline with the breast cancer warriors.
>
> Sorry I don't have any more details, but I'll keep you abreast of everything as soon as I know more. I want to tell you that our faith is rooted in the Lord and that He is our strength. Angel and I are confident of God's wonderful presence in our lives; thus we are holding firmly onto the Word of God, His grace and His promises. So that for now, I ask God to continue giving me the strength and peace which surpasses all understanding to go up the mountain ahead of me and in the way experience His wonderful grace and glory.
>
> I love you and I'm already grateful for your prayers.

While writing those words I realized one more thing, I was determined to fight. I was not going to hide. It had already been too much for one day. I was emotionally exhausted. I waited until the next day to continue "praying" the news.

Sharing the News With Friends and Family

Dealing with Denial

The most difficult part of all this for me was explaining it to someone very close to my heart. Sometimes the person reacted with denial, making me feel that there should be another way to go through with all this, or that the doctors didn't know what they were doing. It was tough when that happened. In those situations, I sometimes retreated from a while or avoided talking about it altogether.

While writing those words I realized one more thing, I was determined to fight. I was not going to hide.

The key thing here was patience. I kept them in my prayers asking God that they could understand and for the Lord to help me get through that struggle as well.

I understand that for the people who really care about you the fact that you are facing cancer is very hard to swallow. They will need time managing and dealing with their emotions just as you do. I decided to give them space to deal with their feelings. It is difficult enough to deal with your own feelings and doubts. If others' feelings and confusion overwhelm you do not lose your balance nor your peace. Kindly request some space and ask to continue the conversation later on.

Make sure you feel comfortable with how your health care provider addresses your questions and how he/she helps you understand new information. This greatly helps to keep your poise when people sow doubt—unintentionally—in you. It is important that you understand that breast cancer treatment is not the same for all the breast cancer patients. There are many variables involved. If you understand this, your loved ones will eventually understand.

Dealing with the Overly Concerned

Another challenge you may find is people who think they understand everything. It could be possible that some people start telling you to "do this" or "do that." Don't get mad at them. They are just concerned about your well-being and recovery. Do your research on their recommendations if you want to and discern the information. You may find helpful tips. But above all, avoid being overwhelmed.

COURAGE UNDER FIRE

You may even face criticism. These people, unwittingly, may make you feel guilty for your cancer because you did or ate "this" or because you stopped doing or eating "that." Put the guilt away from you, it is not healthy, and focus instead on what you can improve. If there are any past actions for which you feel responsible, use those as learning opportunities. It's okay if you need to take a break for yourself. Remember, time is too precious to waste on anger, bitterness or fear.

He Is All I Need

Something happened the first morning after "The Day"—the day I was told I had breast cancer. That morning I got in the car to go to work with many things on my mind. I turned on the engine after doing my prayer and began my drive to work. I was putting my situation in God's hands to get through the day. Being a cancer patient never crossed my mind before. Now here I was, driving to work, feeling the heaviness of the situation on my shoulders and facing that steep mountain in my way. Even the air was hard to breath!

I turned on the radio station "K-LOVE"[2] and listened to "Everything I Need" interpreted by the Christian rock band Kutless.

I don't have to wait to be healed to give God's testimony and be thankful. God is already working in me . . . and I shall not be silent about that!" I just needed to trust Him and to know Him more and more.

Through that song, God was speaking to me. I was listening to every word of it. I was ecstatic. It was no coincidence! God was speaking to me! God was lifting my soul. He was letting me know that He was carrying me in His arms. He was letting me know that in the middle of my situation, my confusion, my uncertainty and my bending knees, He was coming to my rescue.

While the song played, God was letting me know that He was all I needed. I didn't need healing. All I needed I had in Him. "I don't have to wait to be healed to give God's testimony and be thankful. God is already working in me . . . and I shall not be silent about that!" I just needed to trust Him and to know Him more and more.

That song gave me strength and at the same time, it gave me the courage and knowledge of how to tell the news to the rest of my close friends and

Sharing the News With Friends and Family

family. Through sharing the news, I was going to share God's presence by letting them know about this song and how it came to me at that precise moment. I said to many friends, "God is already holding my hand. Please join me in my prayers and in thanksgiving."

Some of my friends asked me if they could share the news of my situation with others. I told them, "By all means do so, if it is to request prayers for me." Little did I know that soon a prayer chain beyond my circle of close friends and family was going to be raised.

Sharing the News With Kids

When I broached the subject with my kids, Alejandro and Gabriel, they were 10 and 8 years old respectively. Alejandro in particular was old enough to realize that something was going on. Maybe he sensed something through the many unusual phone calls going on or because my husband and I were frequently talking in low voice to each other. Maybe it was because the way I started looking at them. I didn't want Alejandro to get the wrong message from something he might have overheard. He was old enough to know that cancer is not good, and that cancer kills. I didn't want him to fear. I had to tell him something. The children soon enough would know that something was wrong.

I remember one time when Alejandro was younger, maybe 4 years old, that he told Angel and me, "You are my favorite parents,"—he made my day! I replied to him, "And you are my favorite older son and Gabriel is my favorite younger son!" Being "his favorite mom" I had to be honest with him and Gabriel and tell them about the situation without scaring them or worrying them and without lying to them. I couldn't exclude them from what was going on. I couldn't divorce them from reality. We were family and we were going to be together in this.

I resolved to sit down with them and tell them about the cancer without using the word "cancer." I had to go slowly with them. I first told them that a doctor found a few bad little cells inside my breast that were harmful. Those little cells were like bad germs contaminating my body and causing harm. I told them that the doctor was going to remove those bad cells from my breast and put them under a microscope to study them further. That way I told the kids that I was going to have breast surgery.

Later on, as the whole panorama was unfolding and I realized that only a surgery was not enough to get rid of the cancer, I shared with them little by little what the treatment process was going to be like. I told them about the changes that would be visible to them and about how those bad cells were trying to hide inside my armpit. I let them know that I was going to be treated well and I tried to be optimistic. I figured that if I was optimistic, they would be too.

Sharing the News With Kids

I remember when I first used the "cancer" word with them. I approached Alejandro to ask him what he knew about cancer—I wanted to know first what exactly he knew about cancer to know how to talk openly about it. Then, when I used the "cancer" word for the first time with Gabriel, I made sure that Alejandro was by his side. Because Gabriel is very attached to Alejandro and is always looking up to his big brother, I wanted them to be together when I first talked about the cancer with Gabriel.

The idea I used to describe the cancer to my sons was that there were enemy cells battling against good ones. They understood that concept. Because we had already talked about bad cells harming the good ones, I told them that when the doctors put the bad ones in the microscope, they were behaving like those that the doctors called cancer cells. I explained to them that because cancer cells were found in my breast, I had breast cancer. I let them know that it was not contagious. I also told them that, thanks to the many years that doctors and scientists had been studying breast cancer, there was much hope for medical treatment and that the early detection and medical advances were saving lives. I wanted them to know that there was hope.

A key thing I was very emphatic about was to call the cancer by its full name: breast cancer. To avoid assumptions that would otherwise cause them stress, I wanted them to understand and use the full name of the cancer in case they wanted to share this with their teachers or someone else. I didn't want them to think that this was a secret. I knew that children share personal things with their teachers and I wanted to give them flexibility and save them from unnecessary stress or feelings of guilt.

In every conversation I prepared them for what was to come regarding my treatment. I looked for examples to help them understand. I encouraged them to ask questions and I was honest with them if I didn't know the answers. I wanted them to know that it was okay if we didn't have all the answers and that we were going to get there step-by-step. I told them that sometimes I was going to feel tired or grumpy, but also told them that all that was going to be temporary. I told them that if they saw me like that, that it was going to be because of the treatment and not because of them. I brought them to the clinic one day so they could meet the medical staff and my doctor.

COURAGE UNDER FIRE

In all our conversations I stressed to them the importance of prayer and faith. Sometimes we prayed together and sometimes I asked them for prayer, letting them know that God listens and that He is with us. I reminded them about a "VeggieTales" song that said "God is bigger than the boogie man, He's bigger than Godzilla and the monsters on TV!"

The time came that I had to tell my kids about the effects of chemotherapy. I knew that the type of chemotherapy I was going to receive had the visible side effect of hair loss. I told them that the doctor was going to give me medication to combat the breast cancer "enemy cells" that were hiding in my body. Because we are all great fans of the film "Star Wars," when talking to my boys I referred to the chemotherapy treatment as the Jedi battle in Episode II of the film series. I told them that it was going to be like that Jedi battle inside me, in which the "the Jedi-swinging lightsabers" (the medication) were going to hit and debilitate some good cells. I explained to them that the medication was going to cause hair loss and make me look sick and weak. Nevertheless, I continuously told them to not fear and that we must trust a mighty God. I encouraged them to pray constantly so that they could also feel the peace and strength of our Lord.

"If you feel scared, give me a hug and let's pray together," I told them.

I told the kids that at some point they would have to help mom and dad by keeping their things in order and helping in little things around the house. I told them that by doing that, they would be a tremendous help.

We were together in this battle. We always looked for the good sense of humor whenever possible and took things in a positive way. We had to. I wanted to live, love and laugh.

While preparing myself for the impact of hair loss, I decided to get a wig before starting chemotherapy—later on I learned that the correct way to refer to the wig was "cranial prosthesis." I felt that having a wig before hair loss made me feel less anxious about the whole issue. One day I told the kids that dad and I were going to shop for a wig. Gabriel couldn't wait to satisfy his curiosity and asked me if I was going to let him try it on to see how it would feel like. We all laughed. I replied that he was going to be the first one to try it on, then Alejandro and finally dad. Afterwards we were going to decide who looked prettier. It was a deal!

Believe me! The time came to enter the wig contest. We took turns wearing the wig. The only rule was: "No picture taking!" Gabriel won. We were together in this battle. We always looked for the good sense of humor whenever possible and took things in a positive way. We had to. I wanted to live, love and laugh.

THE QUESTIONS . . .

The Crossroad

I was determined to fight the good fight with that stupid cancer. I was at a crossroad, a time in which important changes were occurring and major decisions had to be made. I looked upon the Lord for direction and read in Proverbs 1 and Jeremiah 33:

> *Surely I will pour out my spirit on you;*
> *I will make my words known to you.*
> *(Proverbs 1:23, NKJV)*

> *'Call to Me, and I will answer you,*
> *and show you great and mighty things,*
> *which you do not know.'*
> *(Jeremiah 33:3, NKJV)*

I then put my prayers before Him—God was pouring his peace on me:

> "Lord, help me to come to you with a trusting heart laying my petitions in front of you. If I had asked you for direction and for you to talk to my heart, then help me to recognize your voice. Strengthen in me the disposition to live in you and you in me."

> "Lord, may that my biggest challenge in all this be the communion with you and to walk with you. If I don't yet can catch a glimpse of the horizon ahead, please give me enough light to take the next step. Give me the strength and the courage to hold on to you firmly."

More Results Unfolding

I had decided that I wanted the tumor removed right away. My gynecologist helped me find a surgeon. My surgeon helped me found an oncologist. Never before in my life would I have thought that I would need an oncologist.

I had some names of oncologists to interview. I prayed about this a lot. I reduced my list of doctors to interview to three. I called the first one. The woman who answered greeted me kindly and set up an appointment for the next day. I was told that for new patients the doctor liked to spend a long time with them. I was relieved to have an appointment the very next day and with the very first doctor I called.

If I don't yet can catch a glimpse of the horizon ahead, please give me enough light to take the next step. Give me the strength and the courage to hold on to you firmly.

I put the cancer clinic address in my GPS that morning. When approaching the clinic, I realized it was not big. I liked that. I approached the main entry doors while taking a deep breath. When I entered the clinic, the woman at the front desk smiled at me as if she were expecting me. I moved toward the counter and introduced myself.

"Hi Mrs. Rivera, I'm Dorothy, I spoke to you yesterday over the phone."

She told me that Dr. Kazhdan was expecting me but first I needed to complete some paperwork. She gave me a stack of papers to fill out. While filling out all those papers, I paused at a blank space that read "Reason for Visit." I clutched my pen and wrote: "breast cancer."

It was not long before I was asked to go inside to have my vital signs taken. I was then sent to an examination room to wait for the doctor. I soon heard a firm knock on the door.

"You must be Mrs. Rivera!" Dr. Kazhdan said while giving me a big smile.

I stood up to give her a handshake, but she gave me a huge hug instead. She was tall and had a Russian sounding accent. I was short and I had this unique Puerto Rican accent . . . "This is going to be interesting," I thought.

She moved her chair beside mine and looked me in my eyes. Her sincere smile and her presence made me feel comfortable. She asked me kindly:

"Well, Mrs. Rivera what brings you here?"

I shrugged my shoulders while taking a deep breath and I said:

"I guess . . . breast cancer."

"You know, I'm an oncologist not because I like cancer . . . I hate cancer, especially when it is inside the body."

She made me laugh with that comment. I imagine she saw that I was very anxious. I replied as I wiped off a treacherous tear:

"Yes, I hate it too . . ."

"It's okay. Tell me about it," she calmly said.

Afterwards, we just talked. We talked a lot. I think I was there over an hour. I asked so many questions. For each of them, Dr. Kazhdan not only had an answer but also the honesty to tell me that we still had a lot of results to analyze to determine the optimal treatment. She was very knowledgeable and up-to-date on the latest breast cancer research.

I thought I was going to be terrified at that appointment. On the contrary, I felt really comfortable. Dr. Kazhdan didn't sit at the other side of the desk. We talked side by side. She was listening to me. Dr. Kazhdan was talking to me as a person and not as merely a patient. I liked that; that made me feel confident to face the chaos inside and around me. I even laughed sometimes during the conversation. She had an excellent sense of humor. I told her that I had already set my mind on removing my tumor as soon as possible. She understood. She gave me a phone number to call in case I needed to contact her and walked with me back to Dorothy who arranged for an appointment for a few days after the surgery. Dr. Kazhdan gave me another big hug while lovingly looking me in my eyes and said with concern, "Do not disappear, okay?"

I decided Dr. Kazhdan was going to be my oncologist. She was going to receive the results of the second biopsy after the surgery, and we were going to go from there together.

Initially, since the tumor was fairly small, below two centimeters—or at least that was what we thought based on the first biopsy—I chose to have a lumpectomy[1]. I wanted to have that done fast and get the awful cancer out of me at once. However, I knew that with a lumpectomy I might still need radiation treatment to decrease the chances for the cancer coming back.

It is standard procedure during a breast cancer surgery to perform a biopsy on the tumor extracted, the surrounding tissue and the nearby lymph nodes by the underarm. I went through the lumpectomy expecting to remove the fairly small cancerous lump out of my body. Little did I know that the second biopsy was going to be a total unpleasant surprise.

The Crossroad

A few days after the lumpectomy I received a phone call from the oncologist. I was still recovering from the surgical procedure in my house. Dr. Kazhdan wanted to see me to go over the pathology[2] results of the tissue taken out during the surgery. As part of the cancer staging[3], many parameters are analyzed. The lump resulted to be bigger than what the first biopsy showed. According to the results, the margins[4] were still positive. The doctor explained what this meant. In summary, the insidious cancer cells were still there. They had already started "colonizing" the surrounding tissue. This was not good.

On top of that, the cancer cells appeared in the lymph nodes. This particular statement hit me hard. I knew what this meant . . . the vicious cancer had already started moving away from the breast.

This opened up another world of treatment options. This was going to complicate the decision-making process and the way my doctor and I were going to address my treatment. Different emotions and questions were piling up inside me.

"I thought I was in an early stage of breast cancer! I thought it was small! I thought . . . Now, I could be considering a mastectomy[5]. Then if a mastectomy . . . a left side or a bilateral mastectomy?"

That added another issue that was very difficult for me to digest at that moment, the almost sure possibility of chemotherapy. I tried not to cross the bridge before getting to it. I still had to see the doctor to discuss the scenario and to go into more detail regarding my treatment. The doctor spoke to me about another blood test she recommended that would provide more information on how to proceed. There were yet more tests to be done and more results to discuss.

I called Angel to let him know what was going on. He told me he would leave the office before lunch to take me to the doctor in the afternoon. We were worried. While I waited for Angel to get home, a host of thoughts started to invade my mind.

Through this all, I somehow felt strong. I knew God was surrounding me with his peace that went beyond all understanding. I was holding firmly to His cloak. If my feet were weak for an instant, I knew He was going to carry me and hold me by the hand. Sometimes I got scared or worried for my kids . . . I cannot hide that. But even then, I knew that Jesus had them on His magnificent hands and this understanding kept me at peace.

I reminded myself to take one step at a time. Again, the image of Abraham in Genesis 22 going up the mountain with such a heavy burden was in my mind. His faith kept him walking one step at a time knowing that God Almighty was going to provide. With this in mind and between silent tears, I prayed.

Sometimes I got scared or worried for my kids . . . I cannot hide that. But even then, I knew that Jesus had them on His magnificent hands and this understanding kept me at peace.

Barely Surfing through Statistics

My husband and I had a long conversation with my oncologist. Dr. Kazhdan gave us all the attention we needed while trying to understand the pathology results. She answered our questions and explained the benefits of obtaining the necessary results to have all the cards on the table to better decide what treatment was going to be best for me.

It didn't take me long to realize that cancer and statistics go hand-in-hand. While Dr. Kazhdan talked to us, I was trying to assimilate the cancer staging information, research trends and cancer recurrence percentages, cancer treatment versus chances for survival, and a host of other things.

The results showed that the cancer cells were "Grade 3" in the Bloom-Richardson Grading System. The Bloom-Richardson Grading System is used for grading breast cancer on a scale from 1 to 3. My tumor was high-grade and aggressive, meaning that it was growing and spreading quickly. It had already metastasized[6] to my lymph nodes according to what the results of the sentinel lymph node biopsy[7] revealed. The hearing of that word "metastasized" gave me chills.

While listening to this, I was extremely attentive to the doctor, trying to adsorb all the information like a sponge. I didn't want to miss a thing. I wanted to understand every detail to be able to make informed decisions. At the same time, I couldn't stop the anxiety to realize that a raging cancer was lurking its way inside me.

The Crossroad

There remained imaging studies to be done—CTs[8], MRIs[9], bone scan—to rule out the cancer migrating to other parts of my body, including my brain. More questions were piling up, one on top of the other. "What should come first? Should I get my surgery before the imaging? Should I wait? What about radiation and chemotherapy?"

I had another blood sample taken to conduct a BRCA Gene mutation[10] test. This was a voluntary test because it could have serious implications that I had to be prepared to face. This test was to find if I had a particular gene mutation that promoted breast and ovarian cancer as these two are linked according to the latest research. Considering my age and the fact that I had a high-grade cancer, this additional test was going to give us information to help us evaluate the best treatment options. A positive result would mean that I would have a very high chance for breast cancer recurrence and a 60% to 87% risk of developing ovarian cancer.

So far, because of the tissue surrounding the lump revealed cancer, I was going to need more surgery. I was facing mastectomy. Depending on the BRCA gene mutation test, I would get a better idea to help me decide whether to remove one or both breasts, and/or the ovaries to increase my chances of getting rid of the cancer. The testing would take from 2 to 3 weeks. As part of the next step, I not only had to consider getting rid of the cancer, but I also had to focus on the treatment alternatives to minimize its chance of recurrence or adjuvant therapy.

Because the lymph nodes biopsy was positive and because the cancer cells resulted to be a high-grade, I was going to be a candidate for chemotherapy. At this point, I still didn't know if I was going to have radiation therapy. All I knew was that if I was going to go through radiation, it had to be done after the surgery and after the chemotherapy. I would have to see a radiation oncologist once we had all the facts. Also, I had to be looking into breast reconstruction surgery and finding a plastic surgeon. Even the choice of plastic surgery had different alternatives depending on the treatment scenario. It could be done together with the mastectomy or after going through the chemo and radiation.

On top of that, I had to look for more doctors and specialists. I only had been in Texas 10 months! I didn't even have a primary doctor. I just couldn't go out there asking for plastic surgeon and radiation oncologist references like asking for a dentist. I asked my surgeon and my oncologist for references of other doctors and they kindly provided me with a few to give me the chance to meet various doctors and decide. I needed to start assembling my medical health care team. With all the names in front of me, I also prayed. I wanted God to help me throughout the decision making process and with the associated anxiety.

I realized at that moment that the breast cancer treatment was a work in progress; that there is no definitive treatment for any given cancer. There have been many advances, but there are still many unknowns. It is the accumulation of research and gained knowledge about breast cancer itself that determines its treatment.

After that harsh wind of bad news, we went back home. Angel and I were clear on one thing; to keep up the faith. We couldn't hide our anguish but at the same time, we reinforced to each other that our God is a mighty God. Our God provides.

We went together to pick up the kids at school that afternoon. It was a beautiful spring afternoon. It was not yet time to prepare the kids for what was going on. We decided to improvise and rather enjoy life and quality family time together. We asked the kids what they thought about going to fly kites. A unanimous cheerful "Yey!" filled up the car. Thus, that was precisely what we did. We went to buy some kites and then we went to the park to fly kites until sunset.

Staying Afloat

I kept continuously in my mind the image of Peter in Matthew 14:22-31, when he started to walk against all odds on the unsteady waters upon Jesus' command. The strong wind was creating unmerciful waves, and there was Peter walking. Thanks to Peter and to that moment of history, I knew that I needed to have my eyes firm on Jesus and what He could do instead of paying attention to the uncertainty and harsh wind surrounding me. Even if I started sinking, I knew He was going to grab my hand. I needed to remain faithful to be able to taste the glory of the Lord and His promises.

During one of my prayers, I called out the Lord for strength and direction. I was on my knees; not because I was praying, but because I didn't have the strength to stand up and walk. I think that was my first breakdown.

The Crossroad

I was on the floor between the bathroom and the bed. Fear and doubt were hitting me hard and spitting in my face. Anxiety was choking me. I was feeling so alone. I was crying out to the Lord to let me grab his cloak because I knew if I could only grab his cloak I would be saved. I pictured Mark 5:21-32 and the woman fighting against the pressure of the crowd to approach the Lord. By faith she was certain that by only touching the edge of his cloak she would be saved from her condition. I could imagine that during the tortuous and difficult progress toward the Lord, she received the scorn and condemnation of many who considered her impure due to her blood flow. But she continued on her way, not listening to the voices of those many, but following her faith.

> *Even if I started sinking, I knew He was going to grab my hand. I needed to remain faithful to be able to taste the glory of the Lord and His promises.*

Suddenly, the song "Voice of Truth," interpreted by the Christian rock band "Casting Crowns," started playing on the radio. I continued praying and thanking the Lord for that song and for His voice at that precise moment. My cry turned into awe. The song's lyrics reminded me again of Matthew 14:22-31 when Jesus appeared walking on the water to his disciples who were in the small boat being beaten by the strong winds. I had Peter in my mind, walking toward Jesus and being struck by the waves and strong winds to make him doubt. Like Peter, I was fighting doubt; I was fighting disbelief.

The insidious cancer was laughing at me. Doubt and fear were ripping off my clothes yelling at me that it was worthless to fight. Lies of failure and disappointment were telling me that I was never going to win that fight.

The song was still playing on the radio reminding me the words of Jesus saying: *"Do not be afraid"* (Luke 8:50, NKJV). I needed to focus and to hear His voice because He is the voice of truth.

> Jesus *answered, "I am the way and the truth and the life.*
> *(John 14:6, NIV)*

> *My sheep listen to my voice; I know them, and they follow me.*
> *(John 10:27, NIV)*

The Lord was my source of courage and strength. In that battle I had to listen to the Word of God and put my trust in Him and not in other voices.

COURAGE UNDER FIRE

*I consider that our present sufferings are not worth
comparing with the glory that will be revealed in us.
(Romans 8:18, NIV)*

The radio station kept playing other songs. Then, still on my knees, submerged in awe and gratitude, I declared:

"This is for your glory! I am choosing to listen and believe your voice of truth! The voice of my Shepherd, my Lord, my God."

I feel now the urge to tell you to read and understand the first chapter of the book of John in the Bible. Read it either in the New International Version, the New Century Version or in the New Testament Recovery Version. See the revelation; consider and understand the mystery. I cannot do any other thing but worship my God with my life.

Messages and Updates

During that time I received many encouraging messages from friends and family. One of them was from my friend Todd. He was reminding me that God was so much bigger than my circumstances:

> I have been praying for you all day today. There is a song in VeggieTales that says, "God is bigger than the boogie man. He's bigger than Godzilla and the monsters on TV!" I can only imagine what you are going through, but I do know that God is so much bigger and that He is holding you in His arms right now. He will never let you go. Remember, He is whispering your name as the thunder rolls.

I wanted to update a few close friends and family members. Many of them were far away and wanted to show me support. It was difficult to tell them about what was going on without worrying them. I decided, to not only to give them a short overview of the happenings, but also give them some web links to help them better understand breast cancer treatment.

It was really difficult to update my mom and dad. I didn't want to cause them anguish. They were not that versed in computers so it wouldn't mean a thing giving them the web links so they could get information. I wanted to spare them from the anxiety caused by other people's opinions. Therefore, I was trying hard to grasp and learn as much as possible about breast cancer and its treatment to talk to them with confidence and walk them through the process.

I couldn't help but thinking that my parents would see me as their little girl far away out in the dark. I had to pray before talking to them, for both of them and me, so that I could remain calm. In giving them the updates, I gave them reassurance that I was doing all possible to keep myself informed, telling them about my doctors and about how God was great and filling me with a peace beyond our understanding. I wanted them to feel the faith and hope that I was experiencing. It was great to hear that they had me in the prayer list at their church in Puerto Rico and that many loved ones also had me on their prayers.

I had days that I didn't want to talk to anybody and purposely left the phone far away to avoid listening to it and consequently avoid the guilty feeling of not answering it. There were moments that I just felt that by talking to someone it was going to cause more anxiety than help.

"It is okay. Take your time," Angel said to me softly. He must have felt worried that I would fall into a depression.

When God Speaks

*So do not fear, for I am with you; do not be dismayed, for I
am your God. I will strengthen you and help you; I will
uphold you with my righteous right hand.
(Isaiah 41:10, NIV)*

There were many Bible verses and songs that spoke to me, in particular during the first three months dealing with the knowledge of my breast cancer. I say "dealing with the knowledge of my breast cancer diagnosis" because not only I had to manage and assimilate all what was going on, but also manage all the unexpected changes, the constant flow of information on the diagnosis, my work, my family, all the questions (my own and those of others), the constant decision making, the emotions, the uncertainty . . . I could fill an entire page listing the unsavory mix of things and emotions that I was carrying on my shoulders day after day. There were many God's promises to which I held onto. Some of them:

*^{10} if you feed those who are hungry and take care of the needs
of those who are troubled, then your light will shine in the
darkness, and you will be bright like sunshine at noon. ^{11} The
Lord will always lead you. He will satisfy your needs in dry
lands and give strength to your bones. You will be like a
garden that has much water, like a spring that never runs dry.
(Isaiah 58:10-11, NCV)*

*Now to Him who is able to do exceedingly abundantly
above all that we ask or think, according to the power
that works in us,
(Ephesians 3:20, NKJV)*

*But he said to me, "My grace is sufficient for you, for my
power is made perfect in weakness." Therefore I will boast
all the more gladly about my weaknesses,
so that Christ's power may rest on me.
(2 Corinthians 12:9, NIV)*

*^{1} I lift up my eyes to the mountains— where does my help
come from? ^{2} My help comes from the Lord, the Maker of*

heaven and earth. . . . ⁵ The Lord watches over you— the Lord is your shade at your right hand; ⁶ the sun will not harm you by day, nor the moon by night. ⁷ The Lord will keep you from all harm— he will watch over your life; ⁸ the Lord will watch over your coming and going both now and forevermore.
(Psalms 121, NIV)

⁶ Do not be anxious about anything, but in every situation, by prayer and petition, with thanksgiving, present your requests to God. ⁷ And the peace of God, which transcends all understanding, will guard your hearts and your minds in Christ Jesus.
(Philippians 4:6-7, NIV)

I was listening almost every day to the "K-LOVE" Christian radio station. I didn't want to miss a thing of what the Lord wanted to tell me each day or the blessings that he had for me that day. There is a song interpreted by the band "MercyMe," "Word of God Speak," which couldn't illustrate better how I felt at this time. With that song in my mind, I approached the Lord and prayed. I invite you to listen to that song. Many times I didn't know what to pray for or didn't have the words to describe what was in my heart. I hugged my Bible, preparing my heart to listen to Him and asking Him to guide my next step. I was speechless; I was out of words . . . I simply stayed there in His presence. I was still; I was quiet. I was pouring my heart to Him.

That song became a reality in my journey through breast cancer and in my life. I found myself many times out of words in prayer. How is possible to pray without words? All I can say, it's possible. I constantly meditated in God's majesty and God's Word flowed and nourished me. During the breast cancer journey, God spoke to me through his Word, through others' testimony, through my children, through my family, through my friends, through many songs and even through the singing of birds.

Many times my prayer was:

"My exhaustion and praise are yours . . . I don't have anything to offer you, only my heart marked by your love and the joy of the blessings that you have already given me. All I am, in fact, is yours."

His Grace Is Sufficient

I was often listening to the song "Praise You in This Storm" from the band "Casting Crowns." This song talks about the difficult times we face and how we sometimes deeply desire that God would step in and save the day. Somehow, God's reply is not immediate or is not in the way we expect. All we may perceive is that the situation doesn't go away, that the hardship is still there and that we continue walking in the valley of shadows. This may trigger the impression that the Lord is not hearing us, nor responding, or delaying the response we desperately want. He listens and He responds. Sometimes His reply could be "I'm with you. Do not be afraid." Sadly, many times we withdrew long before receiving the blessing He has for us, what He wants to show us; or we get disappointed because we don't recognize His answer for not being what we expected.

> *And God said, "I will be with you . . .*
> *(Exodus 3:12, NIV)*

> *When you pass through the waters, I will be with you; and when you pass through the rivers, they will not sweep over you. When you walk through the fire,*
> *you will not be burned; the flames will not set you ablaze.*
> *(Isaiah 43:2, NIV)*

That reply "I'm with you," is found everywhere in the Bible. It is a constant. Like those words say, you may still be within the rain in the middle of the storm; but be still, be silent to be able to hear Him whispering to you that He won't leave you. He is right there with you to go through the storm with you, to give you strength, to even carry you. Suddenly, the feeling of His magnificent grace just surrounds you and the peace of God, which goes beyond all understanding, guards your heart and your mind.

One of my favorite lines in the "Praise You in This Storm" song is one that refers Psalm 56:8: *"You keep track of all my sorrows. You have collected all my tears in your bottle. You have recorded each one in your book."*

To know that the Lord keeps track of my sorrows, of every tear I've poured, tells me that He cares, that I am not forgotten, that He sees me and that His presence is always there. So although my heart was troubled, I was going to praise Him through the storm. The song repeats the first lines of Psalm 121: "I lift my eyes unto the hills, Where does my help come from? My help comes from the Lord, The maker of Heaven and Earth." Therefore, even in the middle of the Storm you can cry out to Him. Know your God . . . the maker of Heaven and Earth . . . the One who tells you "I'm with you."

Even in the midst of our weakness or in situations that we would like so desperately for God to intervene and take those away from us, He reminds us of His grace. In those situations is when His power may rest on us:

> *But he said to me, "My grace is sufficient for you, for my power is made perfect in weakness." Therefore I will boast all the more gladly about my weaknesses, so that Christ's power may rest on me.*
> *(2 Corinthians 12:9, NIV)*

To me it is amazing when He talks through His Word. He can give you the strength to praise Him with all your heart regardless of your circumstances. You can put your prayers in His hands and let Him surround you with His peace and the knowledge of His love.

> *Do not be anxious about anything, but in everything, by prayer and petition, with thanksgiving, present your requests to God. And the peace of God, which transcends all understanding, will guard your hearts and your minds in Christ Jesus.*
> *(Philippians 4:6-7)*

It is not on our time. The time is His. Let's praise Him in the storm.

THE TREATMENT

On the Verge of a Miracle

I thought about naming this chapter "The Battle Begins," but the truth is that the battle really begins at the moment that one is faced with the cancer diagnosis. It is not just a battle of overcoming the harshness of the breast cancer treatment; it is a battle of faith. Not only was I battling with the direct and associated effects of the treatment (surgery, chemotherapy, radiation), but I was also battling against fear, doubt, isolation, anger, guilt, confusion, anguish and maybe depression and lies of hopelessness.

When I think about those days, I realize that I was each day on the verge of a miracle. God was transforming all my fears and the chaos around and inside me into peace. He was transforming my darkness into light. He was filling my loneliness with his presence. My pain and grief, He was transforming those into joy. In my nakedness and vulnerability, He was clothing me with His love. I was seeing His hand on me. He was making me able to walk through the waters. I was experiencing the direct intervention of the power of God in my life, to me that was a miracle—a miracle occurring day after day after day.

Courage . . . A Definition, an Attitude

A common definition for courage you can find in the dictionary is that courage is the quality of mind or spirit that enables a person to face difficulty, danger or pain, without fear; bravery. I like that definition but I don't agree with the "without fear" remark. I would rather say that courage is the ability to act despite tremendous fear. That means that if you recognize fear daunting you, you can choose to either let fear drive you or choose faith. Choose faith and practice it and let faith drive away fear. God will give you the strength to face your situation and take action.

> *I was determined to be a courageous warrior to face cancer, fear and uncertainty, living every moment and not sit there helpless, feeling sorry for myself . . . I needed to transform the way I looked at myself. This was a constant battle, a battle of faith, an attitude.*

Therefore, I was determined to be a courageous breast cancer warrior, living every moment and not sit there helpless, feeling sorry for myself. I didn't want anybody to feel sorry for me, either. I needed to transform the way I looked at myself. This was a constant battle, a battle of faith, an attitude. I put on the armor of God, Ephesians 6:10-18, NIV:

The Armor of God

^{10} Finally, be strong in the Lord and in his mighty power. ^{11} Put on the full armor of God so that you can take your stand against the devil's schemes. ^{12} For our struggle is not against flesh and blood, but against the rulers, against the authorities, against the powers of this dark world and against the spiritual forces of evil in the heavenly realms. ^{13} Therefore put on the full armor of God, so that when the day of evil comes, you may be able to stand your ground, and after you have done everything, to stand. ^{14} Stand firm then, with the belt of truth buckled around your waist, with the breastplate of righteousness in place, ^{15} and with your feet fitted with the readiness that comes from the gospel of peace. ^{16} In addition to all this, take up the shield of faith, with which you can extinguish all the flaming arrows of the evil one. ^{17} Take the helmet of salvation and the sword of the Spirit, which is the word of God. ^{18} And pray in the Spirit on all occasions with all kinds of prayers and requests. . . .

Sometimes, I was tempted to ask God this question: "Why? Is it something I did?" You have to understand that it is not about why. It is not about what you did. It's about what can you do. It's time to fight. It's time to believe! Look at what the Lord declares in the following verses:

^{1} As Jesus was walking along, he saw a man who had been blind from birth. ^{2} "Rabbi," his disciples asked him, "why was this man born blind? Was it because of his own sins or his parents' sins?" ^{3} "It was not because of his sins or his parents' sins," Jesus answered. "This happened so the power of God could be seen in him.
(John 9:1-3, NLT)

> *Be strong and of good courage; do not be afraid,*
> *nor be dismayed, for the LORD your God*
> *is with you wherever you go.*
> *(Joshua 1:9, NKJV)*

> *For I know the plans I have for you," declares the LORD,*
> *"plans to prosper you and not to harm you,*
> *plans to give you hope and a future.*
> *Then you will call on me and come and pray to me,*
> *and I will listen to you.*
> *(Jeremiah 29:11-12, NIV)*

It is hard to describe, but I often felt as if I were surrounded by a dense fog. In those times, I clutched to my Lord's cloak. Without pause, His embrace held me. Proverbs 3:5-6 (NIV) was on my heart each day:

> *Trust in the Lord with all you heart and lean not*
> *on your own understanding;*
> *in all you ways acknowledge him,*
> *and he will make your paths straight.*

It was not about whether I understood the whole situation or not. It was not about what I knew, but rather *who* I knew. My trust was in the Lord; I leaned on Him.

> *"For my thoughts are not your thoughts, neither are your*
> *ways my ways," declares the Lord.*
> *"As the heavens are higher than the earth,*
> *so are my ways higher than your ways*
> *and my thoughts than your thoughts.*
> *(Isaiah 55:8-9, NIV)*

> *So do not fear, for I am with you;*
> *do not be dismayed, for I am your God.*
> *I will strengthen you and help you;*
> *I will uphold you with my righteous right hand.*
> *(Isaiah 41:10, NIV)*

My Provider

As long as we had been married both my husband and I had full time jobs. While in college our full time job had been studying. After graduating from college we both had full-time paying jobs. God blessed us later with two wonderful kids and our jobs provided a sense of safety . . . salary, health plan, among others.

When I was diagnosed with breast cancer, I had a fairly reasonable "cushion" of accumulated sick leave to use. However, it was not limitless. As the days passed and I was often not able to go to work, my "cushion" was getting depleted. This was very troubling since if I depleted all my accumulated leave, I would be forced to go into a non-pay status and would be unable to pay my health care premiums. If that happened, I would have to apply for a "Leave Donation Program," a list of individuals needing hours of leave to cover for family or health emergencies. Through this program I could keep receiving my salary to continue paying my health care premiums. I would have to rely on other people's leave donations and somehow notify them that I was on the program . . . total uncertainty.

We had some emergency savings, but this money was already being used to take care of out-of-pocket health-related expenses. The cancer was also impacting Angel's job. He was taking care of me, driving me to medical appointments when I couldn't drive and when he was in his office he was pretty much "on-call" in case I had an emergency. He had been in his position for less than a year and with this happening, it was unclear if that job was going to last.

I also worried about my kids, about Angel, about our relationship. Too many things were piling up on top of one another without clear solutions. I tried to live one day at a time, but it was extremely difficult to not be overcome with worry.

It was when I needed Him most that God led me to Mathew 6:19-34 (NCV). It was a passage I knew so well, but you are never done reading God's Word because it speaks to you in different ways at different times.

> [19]*Don't store treasures for yourselves here on earth where moths and rust will destroy them and thieves can break in and steal them.* [20]*But store your treasures in heaven where they*

> *cannot be destroyed by moths or rust and where thieves cannot break in and steal them. ^{21} Your heart will be where your treasure is. . . . ^{25} "So I tell you, don't worry about the food or drink you need to live, or about the clothes you need for your body. Life is more than food, and the body is more than clothes. ^{26} Look at the birds in the air. They don't plant or harvest or store food in barns, but your heavenly Father feeds them. And you know that you are worth much more than the birds. ^{27} . . . Don't worry and say, 'What will we eat?' or 'What will we drink?' or 'What will we wear?' ^{32} The people who don't know God keep trying to get these things, and your Father in heaven knows you need them. ^{33} Seek first God's kingdom and what God wants. Then all your other needs will be met as well. ^{34} So don't worry about tomorrow, because tomorrow will have its own worries. Each day has enough trouble of its own.*

Home, finances, insurance, work and all the rest of the things I was worrying about were unreliable and temporary. No matter what was going on, God was our provider. Psalm 23 was also in my heart, each line resonating with my current situation.

"God alone is my provider. So in Him I shall rest."

My family was in His hands, my kids were in His hands; He was taking care of them. No better hands than His to hold them! He was taking care of me. I couldn't add another hour of life by worrying. I couldn't put my trust in a temporary cushion; I had to let go. I had to let go of my children and my husband to free myself from the fear of loss and to avoid the frustration of not having control of the situation.

> I had to let go of my children and my husband to free myself from the fear of loss and to avoid the frustration of not having control of the situation.

"It's not about what I know but about <u>who</u> I know. God will provide," I kept repeating to myself.

On the Verge of a Miracle

This understanding gave me the peace I needed and the strength to fight. It gave me the certainty to tell my children not to worry because God knows our needs, He sees things that we don't see, and He takes care of us.

"Father, lead me through this process," I prayed.

> *How precious are your thoughts about me, O God.*
> *They cannot be numbered!*
> *I can't even count them;*
> *they outnumber the grains of sand!*
> *And when I wake up, you are still with me!*
> *(Psalm 139:17-18, NLT)*

The Surgeries

I expected my first surgery—the lumpectomy—to remove the cancerous lump from my body. I don't remember much of that day. I remember waiting with my kids and husband and then waking up in the recovery room. After the surgery, as I was waking up from the anesthesia, I was feeling a little sore. I recall a very nice and sweet voice saying, "Oh, she's waking up. I'm going to call your husband and kids." The sweet voice said a few other things, I think, but I can't remember. There was light, but almost everything was blurry.

I heard my husband's voice and the voices of my two little ones greeting me. With time, I realized that the sweet voice I had heard upon first awakening was that of my nurse. She was telling my kids and my husband that she, too, was a breast cancer warrior. She was going through her treatment. She was making light hearted jokes to me, my husband and my kids about her wig and her appearance. She even took her wig off at one point. With her jokes and our laughter, she was showing me that it was not only about cancer, it was about attitude and keeping my perspective.

With her attitude, she was reassuring me that all this was temporary; that this was just a stage, a phase. I was still recovering, waking up from the anesthesia. I was starting to feel a little bit more the soreness of the surgery. Some things were still unclear. But one thing I remember very clearly . . . her candid smile and my kids laughing with her.

> *With her jokes and our laughter, she was showing me that it was not only about cancer, it was about attitude and keeping my perspective.*

How wonderful God is to place her that day on our path!

Getting Ready for the Second Surgery

Not long after the first surgery, my doctor discussed the pathology results with me. The margins were still positive, meaning that the cancer cells had already started to colonize the surrounding tissue. Knowing that I had a very aggressive cancer and that it had metastasized to my lymph nodes, I didn't

The Surgeries

want to wait for the imaging tests. All that remained were the results from the BRCA gene mutation test.

The results of the BRCA gene mutation test would give us a better idea of whether to remove one or both breasts and the ovaries to decrease the chances of cancer recurrence. After almost three weeks, the results came back negative. That was truly good news!

As part of the next step, I not only had to consider how to rid my body completely of cancer, but also the treatment alternatives to minimize its chance of recurrence. I took some weeks to think about the test results and to do my Internet research to formulate more questions and concerns to discuss with my doctor.

I was convinced of what I wanted to do next, but I first wanted to discuss it with Angel. One of the things he told me was that no matter what he thought, he was not going to feel right telling me what to do or not do with my own body. He pointed out that he was married to me and not to my breasts. He reassured me that no matter what I decided, whether to keep one breast, whether to get rid of them both, whether to have implants or not, he was going to stand by me. He told me:

"You are you. You are not your breasts or the way you look."

I told him what I wanted to do. He gave me a big hug. He said that if I was doing that to improve my chances of survival, he was glad because he wanted to be with me for many years to come. We shared some tears and then he added:

"Don't forget to remind me before the surgery, so I can kiss them both good bye!" Then we shared a big laugh.

The time came for me to discuss my options with my oncologist. Dr. Kazhdan empowered me with information to guide me in the decision making process, but the final decision would be mine. I have read that before it was not this way and this is evidence of the advances made in cancer treatment in recent years.

"So Mrs. Rivera, what have you decided?" Dr. Kazhdan asked me.

"I decided to go with a mastectomy," this was hard to say.

"Left side or both breasts?" she asked again.

"Both," I replied—this reply was even harder than the first one.

She hugged me. Dr. Kazhdan would never hesitate to give you a hug. Somehow she always had a beautiful big smile and a magic box full of compliments for each patient. She had the kind of voice that makes you feel her charming presence down the hallway, and you smile because you know that soon you will receive free hugs, smiles and a lot of compliments.

I told her that because there was a possibility of radiation treatment after the chemotherapy, my plastic surgeon was recommending delayed reconstruction to avoid damaging the implants. Therefore, I chose to go with the temporary breast tissue expanders[1] to be placed immediately after the mastectomy during the same surgery. My doctor was going to coordinate the surgery with the general surgeon and the plastic surgeon. I wanted to have the surgery as soon as possible so I could recover and start the chemotherapy.

My prayer those days while preparing myself mentally for the mastectomy was:

> "Lord take me in your hands, keep me safe. Be in that room with all the surgeons and doctors. Lead them in wisdom. Even if I'm asleep, strengthen my soul and spirit. My worship and praise to the God of my life. It doesn't matter where I am, You will be with me."

I was also thanking God for his presence and for being *"bigger than the boogie man, bigger than Godzilla and any monster on TV!"*

The Emotional Challenge

Those few weeks after the mastectomy were really rough. I was given a device to do breathing exercises a few times a day. I also had to do arm exercises regularly to recover the mobility of my arms. They always left me fatigued and struggling to catch my breath. It was difficult to sleep. It wasn't easy to find a comfortable sleeping position due to the pain and because of the surgical drain tubes still inserted in my body. I couldn't wait to have the tubes removed! I also didn't want to overuse the pain medication—which was very strong. I didn't want to become dependent, but there were some days that I

The Surgeries

had no choice. My parents came from Puerto Rico to help us for a while, but then they had to leave.

My recovery was slow. I had to exercise patience. It was very hard even to dress myself because of the limited movement of both of my arms after the surgery. I was not prepared for that. All those days and weeks in which I was not able to do much Angel was helping me day and night. I sometimes got worried about him. "Will he get tired?" I thought. Then I prayed for him, for God to fill him with strength and peace. He was getting the kids ready in the morning, getting their breakfast ready, pretty much taking care of the house, the kids, himself and me all at once. He was also making lunch and dinner during the weekends or buying meals if he got tired of cooking. He was buying the groceries, maintaining the cars, working, driving me to appointments and even working at nights to complete projects at work that he couldn't complete during the day. He was taking a lot of time off from work to help me. I feared that this was impacting his job he started less than a year ago. I worried about how long he was going to withstand this entire situation.

I was often frustrated because I couldn't help him with everyday chores around the house: cooking, laundry, shopping—and I wanted to help. When I tried to help, there was not much I could do without getting fatigued. I wondered, "When will I be able to work…to do things at home, to drive, to cook and carry things without them being too heavy to handle?" I couldn't even get the milk jug out of the refrigerator! "When I could be useful again or productive?"

I was aware that "Mrs. Depression" was stalking me. I realized that I was not being fair to myself by thinking those things, but that didn't help. I was feeling so useless . . . as a mom . . . as a wife. We were already swamped by everyday things and I had not even started chemotherapy. Angel was doing so much in the house, trying to keep the kids busy and away from me to let me rest. Many times I felt that everyone in the house but me was engaged, that all of them were going on without me and I couldn't help but feel isolated. I couldn't help but wonder if Angel would get tired of all this and I worried about the impact this could have in our relationship.

One thing I have learned through my years of marriage is that in a relationship, I'm responsible not only for what I say but also for what I assume and don't share. We were going through so much already. That was why it was so important to communicate, to talk about each other's fears with honesty no matter how uncomfortable it was. I resolved to share my thoughts and feelings of helplessness and frustration with Angel.

I told him with sadness how useless I felt and how much I worried about him. He covered my lips and said:

"Hey, shut up. I'm here. Be strong. You need rest to be able to fight. I'm fighting with you. God is our strength. He will provide," he said.

"Yes I know. God will provide," I replied.

Angel told me that he knew that this situation was temporary and that God was giving him the strength to fight with me. He reminded me how I took care of him for four months when he had an accident that left him unable to walk, and that now it was his turn. He told me that he would not abandon me nor would he distance himself from me. He told me that my health was more important than his job; that if anything happened, God was going to provide.

To avoid feeling isolated we agreed that if I wanted some space I was going to request it and that he would not assume the kids would accidentally hurt me by playing near me. I told him I needed to see the kids running and jumping around me and that I would show them how to be careful around "Mom." I asked him to let me at least help with small things like sorting the laundry to feel helpful. We were going to figure this out together, step by step.

> We wanted to show our kids a better world and the importance of caring for each other. We all were going to engage in whatever task we had, in communication, in helping each other, even sometimes leaving the housework undone to have time for one another.

Then we hugged each other. I acknowledged my weakness and faced my fears. I had to be honest to myself and put myself in God's hands so that the power of God could shine in me. I reassured myself:

"God will help me through this . . . Oh yes! He will carry us through this!"

The Surgeries

We wanted to show our kids a better world and the importance of caring for each other. We all were going to engage in whatever task we had, in communication, in helping each other, even sometimes leaving the housework undone to have time for one another.

The Third Surgery

The third surgery was minor. I was going to have an infusion port implanted near my collarbone that was going to be used for chemotherapy. The infusion port was attached to a flexible silicone catheter that was threaded intravenously for long-term venous access for infusion of medications. The infusion port could be left in place for months to preclude me from many needle sticks in the arm.

Though this was going to be a minor surgery, I was still anxious. The thought of the unknown and of facing chemotherapy made me feel uneasy. My oncologist offered my husband and me a chemotherapy orientation to learn about the treatment, about the drugs I was going to take, about the side effects and how to manage those. As part of the orientation Nurse Amber took us on a tour of the clinic. We visited the laboratory, the infusion room, and were introduced to the staff. The nurses gave us pamphlets to read and a nutrition book to help me cope with the side effects of chemo. All the information helped us to minimize the anxiety, but despite this, with the days approaching my first chemotherapy session, I was getting more nervous.

To my surprise, the nurse that was in the recovery room during my first surgery was there in the preparation room. My husband recognized her and called out to her letting her know we remembered her and that we cherished the memories we had from her last visit. She stopped by my bed with a big smile and shared with me the news that in a week she was going to be done with chemo. Curious thing, I was just getting ready to have mine. By the time we met, I didn't know that I was going to have to go through chemo because we didn't have the results of the sentinel lymph node biopsy. I told her about the mastectomy and about the events after the first surgery and that I was getting the infusion port that very day.

I thought she saw in my eyes some of the uncertainty of what was to come, but also hope. She gave me a big and long hug.

"I know how you are feeling. Everything will be all right. You hang in there," she said.

"Oh . . . you look beautiful," she added with her hug.

She also hugged my husband and then left. I was in the bed, still in the prep room, with the curtain closed and alone with my thoughts for a while. Angel came back, kissed me and told me, "The anesthesiologist is coming."

After that, there was the smile of the anesthesiologist . . . the speech about the anesthesia . . . then my thoughts again, and the anesthesia administration. I was repeating Psalm 23 in my mind. I remember light, some movement, a subtle smile with my eyes to Angel . . . and then, I was out.

Carpe Diem

Once I saw a movie, *Dead Poets Society*, in which a teacher inspires his students and explains the phrase "carpe diem." This Latin phrase means "seize the day." That phrase stuck with me during my breast cancer fight journey.

Instead of worrying about my kids, their future, about the uncertainty ahead, I chose to enjoy life and cherish life with them. I found inspiration meditating on the many blessings that God had given me. I started seeing my kids not as mine but as His. They were a gift to me, fragile blessings to nurture, love and lead. Meditating on the many blessings God had given me helped me to smile by reminding me of the many moments of our lives together that I had recorded in a journal many years before. Whenever I was feeling blue, I took that old journal and read. Those short and simple journal entries helped me feel joy and fed me during the battle with cancer. I share those with you in sections titled *"Remembering."* The reading of those lines gave me another motivation; I found myself writing again. Through writing, I discovered an internal courage, a power beyond my understanding that kept me going, a fire that gave me the strength to battle pain, fear, doubt, isolation, anger, guilt, confusion, anguish and hopelessness. The thoughts I had during my journey through breast cancer I will present in sections titled *"Journal Entry."* I had nothing to offer my Lord but the joy of the blessings He had given me. Cancer was not going to stand in my way to "seize the day."

> *I started seeing my kids not as mine but as His. They were a gift to me, fragile blessings to nurture, love and lead.*

Remembering

I see the kids playing together or having a conversation, and I remember one day when Gabriel was 4 years old. He asked Alejandro: "'*Aleh*' is it true I am your friend? Right . . .?"

It was so important for him that Alejandro was his friend, not only his brother. I thank the Lord for them!

Journal Entry

"Mom, when will you be ready to do stuff again?" Alejandro asks me.

"Well this morning I was able to get you to a birthday party although I still have these uncomfortable drain tubes attached to me from the surgery. I'm getting better I guess. What would you like to do?"

"It would be nice if we could go to the pool, like the other day. Over there you can get some sun if you like. You watch us from the outside. I'll take care of Gabriel and won't let him go deep," he replies.

"I don't promise you anything, but put on your bathing suit and get two towels. Tell Gabriel, as well. Be ready. As soon as I feel ready, we'll go."

I rested for a bit. After a while, I looked through the window and the day was too perfect to not enjoy. I was still feeling a little bit sore. I thought, "Vitamin D, research says, it's good to fight breast cancer. So Vitamin D we will get with a little bit of sun."

"Let's go to the pool!" I said aloud. "Are we ready?"
"YEY!" I heard the boys celebrating.

Journal Entry

I used to stay at home with the kids for their birthdays when they were smaller to show them that they were important to me. On that day, we would plan something fun to do.

One day, I stayed home with both of my kids to celebrate Gabriel's 4th birthday. We danced and laughed. I covered every inch of his little face with kisses. Then, I announced them we were going to Toys R Us to get a gift for Gabriel and a "little something" for Alejandro. That earned me a bunch of hugs that added to the ones I already received by staying with them.

Thank you Lord for that memory! Those of memories inspire me and give me the motivation to keep fighting.

COURAGE UNDER FIRE

> ***Journal Entry***
>
> Witnessing Another Day
>
> Another lily opened today. And I witnessed it!

"Carpe diem" doesn't mean to jump from a plane with a parachute or bungee jump from a bridge. It doesn't mean that you have to let go of your inhibitions and do something risky. It's about appreciating the simple things around you and taking charge with joy of the things that matter. What inspires you? What moves your heart?

Chemo Starts

"Keep breathing . . . One step at a time."

When you read about chemotherapy[1] the first thing you learn is that the goal of chemotherapy is to destroy cancer cells, which divide rapidly. As the chemo wipes out fast growing cells, it can also damage fast growing healthy cells. During chemo orientation and through reading I learned that the damage to healthy blood cells was going to be reflected in side effects such as anemia, fatigue, and risk for infection. Those were some of the reasons why I was going to be monitored constantly during the chemotherapy.

Chemotherapy can also damage the cells of the mucus membranes throughout the body, for example the mouth, throat and stomach. Some typical side effects are mouth sores, diarrhea, and other problems with the digestive system. I was given a long list of medications to help me bear the side effects. It is important that you understand that cancer treatment is not the same for all cancer patients. The same applies to chemotherapy. Not all the chemotherapies are the same for a given cancer. There are many variables involved. It is not my intention here to discuss scientifically how chemotherapy works or it's side effects. I will simply tell you about my experience with chemo and my journey through it.

The Close Encounter

The day came to start my first chemotherapy session. Although I was mentally prepared to start my chemo, I was very concerned that day. I had heard so many bad chemotherapy stories before that I tried to shutdown all I had heard about it and focus instead on being well and strong. I read the pamphlets the doctor gave me about the treatment. I had seen the infusion room and the laboratory. I had prepared my pantry at home with some ingredients that would be helpful to have because I studied the book that the doctor gave me, "Eating Well Through Cancer"[2]. I was getting physically and mentally ready. Still, I couldn't help to feel nervous about what was about to happen.

When we arrived, Dorothy, the receptionist, greeted Angel and me. We sat in the waiting room that felt like a home-like environment. While talking

Chemo Starts

to Dorothy, my nervousness started to abate. After a short wait Dr. Kazhdan approached and told us it was time to go in.

The doctor greeted us with her characteristic big smile and hug. Amber, the nurse who provided the chemo orientation to both of us, greeted me the same way. Amber introduced me to the other nurse, Elizabeth, who was going to check my infusion port. Elizabeth checked my infusion port and declared it "beautiful." She had a blood sample taken through my "beautiful" port and in about 20 minutes later she told me I was ready. "Ready?" I guess I was ready. She told me to take my anti-nausea medication.

These two nurses, Amber and Elizabeth were taking care of all the patients in that infusion room so attentively and kindly. Both were doing so many things at the same time, and they seemed to love what they were doing. They didn't seem annoyed by the infusion pumps' alarms beeping every so often. With patience and a little bit of humor they were taking care of business. Maybe for them, they were just doing their job with dedication. To me, they were making a difference. Their dedication, their attention, their time, their affection, made the difference for me. Instead of being terrified, they made me feel calm, confident and pampered. I felt that I was in good hands. I felt that both Amber and Elizabeth were caring for me as a person, not just as another patient. Amber seated me in a very comfortable motorized recliner, then left to prepare my chemo "cocktail."

I sat in the recliner and played with the controls while smiling at my husband. I was moving it up and down, back and forth—I was just being silly. Angel was laughing at me. I heard Elizabeth say, "Hey, someone is playing with the chair!" and smiled—Oops! She got me. Then Amber approached with the medication and explained to me each of the steps of the treatment carefully. First she was going to give me an infusion of medication to prepare me for the side effects of the chemo. Immediately afterwards, I would be given the chemo itself. My duty was to stay relaxed and let her know if I felt anything unusual. Then the infusion started.

Thoughts started to intrude in my mind. I asked myself, "How long I could be without being able to go to work? How much was I going to last being paid with my accumulated days for sick leave and vacation without having to be on leave without pay?" I had already spent quite a few weeks due to the medical appointments, previous surgeries and recovery. Everything was blurred, as if I was going to enter a path obscured by a dense fog. I had a book with me to read and think about something else for a while. However, it was hard to focus. I tried to rest and I reminded myself to keep breathing . . . "Yilda, one step at a time."

After we left the clinic, we slowly walked to the car. Once inside, while turning on the engine, Angel looked at me as if trying to read my eyes to see how I was feeling, and he gave me a smile. I replied back to him with a weak smile and turned on the radio. I put on the "K-LOVE" radio station and during the way home they started playing "You Never Let Go" by Matt Redman. While listening to that song, I held on to each word. Even if I was swamped by chaos, my Lord was holding me strong. My world was spinning crazy around me but I knew that God was in control. That song ministered me in that moment and beyond and brought to mind Isaiah 41:13, NIV:

> *For I am the Lord your God who takes hold of your right hand and says to you, Do not fear; I will help you.*

While listening to that song, I thanked the Lord because His love was bigger than my situation. He was holding my hand and not letting go.

In the Valley of Shadows . . . An Attitude Toward Difficulty

When we face difficult situations, we can either ask "why?" and bump our heads against the wall or we can view those situations as another way to exercise faith and grow in the knowledge of the Lord's grace. Whatever your struggle may be or the storm you may be facing, the Lord in His grace has promises for you.

> [7] *But we have this treasure in jars of clay to show that this all-surpassing power is from God and not from us.* [8] *We are hard pressed on every side, but not crushed; perplexed, but not in despair;* [9] *persecuted, but not abandoned; struck down, but not destroyed.* [10] *We always carry around in our body the death of Jesus, so that the life of Jesus may also be revealed in our body...* [16] *Therefore we do not lose heart. Though outwardly we are wasting away, yet inwardly we are being renewed day by day.* [17] *For our light and momentary troubles are achieving for us an eternal glory*

> *that far outweighs them all.*
> *(2 Corinthians 4:7-17, NIV)*

When I read these verses I prayed: "My Lord give me understanding to comprehend your Word and to know when you speak to my soul. In receiving you, I receive your life. Show me to understand the purpose of any storm or harsh wind in my life, so that instead of avoiding them, I decide to carry with joy the certainty that together with your life, I will experience in growth your renovating power through it."

> *Then you will call, and the Lord will answer;*
> *you will cry for help, and he will say: Here am I. . . .*
> *(Isaiah 58:9, NIV)*

I can't count how many times I asked the Lord to guide me, to give me strength. In the middle of the valley of shadows, He replied so wonderfully:

> *[4] Let him lead me to the banquet hall, and let his banner over*
> *me be love. [6] His left arm is under my head,*
> *and his right arm embraces me.*
> *(Song of Solomon 2:4, 6, NIV)*

"Thank you my Lord for the certainty of your presence. Guard my heart and mind from anxiety . . . lead my steps."

I wrote before that in my battle with breast cancer, faith was my shield, the Word of God my sword and prayer my food. Many times in prayer, it was like a conversation. God was sustaining me through His Word.

The Word of God is always speaking. Feel the beauty of His love that surrounds you, that fills every space and every gap. In the midst of the dry wind beating my face I fell onto my knees and prayed:

"Thank you Lord because even if I feel insufficient, frustrated and/or overwhelmed by my circumstances, your love snuggles me, feeds me and heartens me."

> *When you pass through the waters, I will be with you;*
> *and when you pass through the rivers,*
> *they will not sweep over you. When you walk through the fire,*
> *you will not be burned; the flames will not set you ablaze.*
> *(Isaiah 43:2, NIV)*

COURAGE UNDER FIRE

In the middle of the storm, I held on to God's promises. Hold on to His Word. Seek Him with your heart, soul and mind and you shall find.

"If there is a storm surrounding me, Lord, show me your peace and sustain me in it."

> [6] *Do not be anxious about anything, but in every situation,*
> *by prayer and petition, with thanksgiving,*
> *present your requests to God.*
> [7] *And the peace of God, which transcends all understanding,*
> *will guard your hearts and your minds in Christ Jesus.*
> *(Philippians 4:6-7, NIV)*

The Battle Continues

The secondary effects of the chemo were felt immediately. Every time I went in for treatment, the doctor gave me additional medication to fight the side effects. Never before had I been forced to carry a bag full of medications. Each one of them had a unique purpose and an order in which to take them. I was told to drink around 64 ounces of non-caffeinated fluids per day, which among other things, would help minimize fatigue and dehydration. I was given a special toothpaste and mouthwash to avoid mouth sores.

I thought I was in fairly good shape to withstand the treatment because of all the athletics and sports I used to be involved in with my kids. I used to practice soccer, tennis and take martial arts. I thought that was going to help in fighting the side effects of the chemo. It turned out that my body didn't have any option but to give in. I was so weak that sometimes I could barely lift my head. The energy was just not there. Even so, I was eager to make all my appointments, stay on schedule and get that cancer treatment behind me.

Many times when I was feeling uncomfortable, I hugged myself and thought "God is control." Then I felt His voice telling me, "Do not fear, I'm with you." I then surrendered myself to His presence and waited for his strength to lift me up.

The walk was not easy, both emotionally and physically, but the Lord was wonderful in demonstrating His restoring power. I kept on fighting the good fight knowing that "faith is the confidence in what we hope for and the assurance about what we do not see" (Hebrews 11).

Under His Wings

I remember one of my first prayers when I was diagnosed with breast cancer: "If I shall walk this path . . . my Lord, lead me. Hold me in your arms. I am self-emptying, so that I can be filled with your revelation."

My anxiety was calmed with the peace of God that transcends all understanding. It was guarding my heart and mind. Little by little, I found myself surrendering my will, my strength, my concerns, my family, my kids to the One who reached me, to the One who loves me. All the blessings I had were in fact wonderful gifts He gave me through His grace. All I was was His. Like Psalm 91, He was covering me with his feathers and under his wings I found refuge.

As the fears subsided, I found myself surrounded by his wings and the first lines of Psalm 23 (NIV) filled me entirely: "The LORD *is* my shepherd; I shall not want."

"He is my shepherd, the good shepherd who takes care of his sheep. He protects his flock, He will protect me, He will protect my family, He will protect my children. The rest . . . I will keep discovering."

It was amazing how the Lord led me. On one occasion I was meditating on a devotional from Charles Spurgeon about Deuteronomy 5:24. I came across the following passage that deeply touched my heart:

> *They who navigate little streams and shallow creeks, know but little of the God of tempests; but they who "do business in great waters," these see his "wonders in the deep.". . . Thank God, then, if you have been led by a rough road, it is this which has given you your experience of God's greatness and loving kindness. Your troubles have enriched you with a wealth of knowledge to be gained by no other means, your trials have been the cleft of the rock in which Jehovah has set you, as he did his servant Moses, that you might behold his glory as it passed by. Praise God that you have not been left to the darkness and ignorance which continued prosperity might have involved, but that in the great fight of affliction, you have been capacitated for the outshinings of his glory in his wonderful dealings with you.*[3]

I was speechless when I read that. I felt I had to praise the Lord who was leading me through the rough road. He was showing me "wonders in the deep." I was experiencing God's greatness and loving kindness, and I was not yet done. I felt awesome and inspired. I still had a lot to share with the world.

Coping With Frustration

Often in the morning I awoke feeling exhausted. How could that be? I slept well but my energy level remained so low. I kept a bottle of water beside my bed to stay hydrated and try to fight the fatigue. "Maybe if I get up and dress, I will feel better and go to work for a few hours," I told myself.

I sometimes thought about going to work and take it easy. I would go to my closet to get dressed and start preparing myself as if it were a normal day only to realize that I didn't have the energy to work or even to drive to work. After a few steps I started gasping and my body felt like melting over my feet. I felt like a wet rag. The only thing I could do was to call the office and tell them I was not going to make it that day. It was frustrating, to realize that I was not even able to do simple tasks.

Even the climb back upstairs to bed was a challenge. The exhaustion and fatigue produced by chemotherapy was like nothing else I had experienced. Sometimes I crawled up the stairs taking me a rest after each step, a rest to recover and regain enough energy to go up the next step. My little dog Windy accompanied me and used to sit beside me and wait while I stared at the wall. Because of this, I came up with the idea to decorate that big, blank wall of the stairway. I decided to put on that empty canvas things that meant something to me and would give me encouragement while facing the struggle of the stairs. I started editing and printing family pictures, old and recent. I chose the ones that left me speechless and made me smile. I was motivated. I took this job very seriously. My "art and interior design" project was not only a source of motivation, but also a short-term goal I knew I could accomplish.

One day, soon after I hatched my plan to decorate the stairway, I felt I had enough energy to do some shopping. Angel probably thought I was crazy to make him drive me to the shopping center to buy picture frames and wall decoration before picking up the kids at the summer camp. I was thinking about the pictures to choose, the orientation of the picture and the frames that would make it all fit together. After choosing a few frames, I saw something that I didn't hesitate to buy; a wall art decoration, about a meter in length, made of metal and glass with a message. I decided that it was going to go at the top of the stairs, facing me as I climbed.

Coping With Frustration

It took me just a few days to complete my project. The kids helped me select the pictures and put them into three large frames. Angel had the task to mount them on the wall. At the bottom of the stairs, the largest part of the wall, I placed a vertical frame that listed the "Fruit of the Spirit": Love, Joy, Peace, Patience, Kindness, Goodness, Faithfulness, Gentleness, Self-control (Galatians 5:22-23). Below that I put a metal wall decoration with the words "Love—Live—Laugh" to inspirit me for the difficult task ahead of climbing the stairs. Along the wall going up the stairs were the three large frames with the family pictures my kids and I selected. That way, when I had to stop and take a rest to catch my breath, I would be looking not at an empty wall, but at images and moments that brought me joy and inspiration. At the top of the stairs I put that piece of art that had caught my eye when I went shopping the materials from my project. It's message read:

> Life is not measured by the amount of breaths we take,
> but by the moments that take our breath away.

The frustration of not being able to do day-to-day activities and simple tasks because of exhaustion, I replaced it with joy and inspiration. Many times I just sat there on the steps to look at the wall or do some reading. I could say that I had lived through many moments that took my breath away and yet, I still had a lot to live, love and laugh. There were so many reasons to keep fighting and to not give up.

Angel and the kids loved the wall! Today, I still look at that wall and remember. It continues to inspire me and makes me smile.

Remembering

I remember that after a very frustrating day at work I picked up the kids from the Daycare Center. I was very silent and submerged in my own thoughts while driving. Suddenly Alejandro, who was then 4 years old, asked me:

"Mom, are you silent?"
"Yep," I answered.
"Because I'm sleeping?"
"Maybe," I replied.
"But I have my eyes open. Look."

I looked in the rearview mirror and I saw these two big and beautiful eyes, wide open looking at mine. He smiled.

"Look at those little eyes, how pretty they are!" I said while smiling back at him.

"But your little eyes are prettier than mine," he replied.

"Alejandro, you make me so happy."

~.~

Journal Entry

Those kinds of memories made me stronger. They made me determined to fight back and be focused. Made me determined to be strong; and to be able to be strong, I was putting myself in the hands of God.

One Day at a Time

Sometimes I felt good and sometimes I didn't. At work, for instance, when I was planning a meeting for the following week, someone might ask me if I was going to be there. I couldn't make time commitments, so I would shrug and politely tell them that if I couldn't make it, my backup would be there. I had a backup, and a backup of the backup, to ensure my projects keep moving along.

The roller coaster of ups and downs, unexpected turns and the inability to plan for the next few days ahead, were also a source of frustration. Even with the family and friends, I couldn't either make commitments to go out somewhere or get together. Sometimes I was able to do things at home, sometimes not. Sometimes I was able to help the kids with schoolwork, but sometimes not.

Many times I had to ask Alejandro to help Gabriel study or to help him maintain his focus to complete his homework. Third grade was proving difficult for Gabriel and sometimes it was very frustrating for me to not be able to help him as much as I wanted to. As a mother, this was incredibly frustrating for me. I prayed for my kids constantly and placed their well being in God's hands. There were times that I was too exhausted to talk and I simply sat with them and watched them while they completed their schoolwork. Sometimes, to help Gabriel practice his reading, I told him to read aloud to me to make me feel better. That seemed to motivate him, and me.

Often, housework overwhelmed us. If I was feeling well for the moment I would tell Angel, "Forget about the housework! Let's do something different. Let's improvise."

Every time when frustration showed up at the door again, I reminded myself to take one day at a time and to count my blessings.

Coping with Hair Loss

*"No more hair brushing, hair styling, or bad hair days
for a while! Welcome hats, headscarves,
wigs, wind and sun!"*

Hair loss was one of the primary side effects of my chemotherapy. The hair roots, or follicles, are fed by fast growing cells and these fast growing cells were going to be targeted by the chemo. Because of that, I knew that sooner or later I was going to face hair loss. I knew from my doctor and nurses that the hair loss was not going to be immediate; it could take two to three weeks after the first dose of chemo.

I had had long hair most of my life. I couldn't visualize myself without hair. Just the thought of that made me feel apprehensive. I suppose that for a woman, her hair is a part of who she is and how she presents herself to the world. Therefore, instead of waiting for my hair to fall off, I decided to cut it short and to donate it to "Locks of Love." Locks of Love is a non-profit organization that provides hairpieces to financially disadvantaged children and youth in the United States and Canada suffering from long-term medical hair loss. That decision helped me feel that I was in control of my future hair loss and moreover, the thought of a child benefiting from my loss made me feel happy.

I went to a hair styling school to have my haircut so that I could also benefit a hair styling student—something that I would have never done before. The student was a little scared as my cut was going to be his first short-style haircut. He constantly requested reassurance, guidance and supervision from his teacher. I encouraged him by cheering him on, "You can do it!" Meanwhile, I was worried and thinking that if the short-style haircut didn't come out right, I would have my wig (cranial prosthesis) as a backup. In fact, I had the wig in the trunk of the car.

My kids occasionally checked up on me. They knew that their mom, who they had always known had long hair, was cutting it short because she was preparing herself for hair loss. They also knew that a child would benefit from my loss. The understanding of that made them experience the curious mixture of joy in the midst of adversity.

Hair loss was one of the first things I discussed with my kids when I knew that I was going to go through chemotherapy. I wanted them to know what was going to happen to me so they wouldn't be scared. I made sure they understood that the hair loss was going to be temporary. I encouraged them to ask questions and if I didn't know the answers, I told them we would find them out together.

My kids also knew that I was probably going to lose my eyebrows and eyelashes, too. I told them that if any of their friends at school asked them about what was going on with their mom to tell them that their mom was fighting cancer and that she was a warrior.

One day Alejandro came home with a painting of a pink ribbon that one of his friends made for me. Within the ribbon were the words: "Breast cancer, fight for the cure." This was a beautiful detail and I still have that painting displayed in a very prominent place in our home.

Journal Entry

Little Hands

I remember when the kids were smaller and how we used to cross the street together holding hands. I was holding Gabriel's hand and Gabriel was holding Alejandro's.

Now they are holding mine. I don't know if they know how much they are helping me to get through this. Their little hands are helping me by holding my hands to make this journey.

Hair Pain?

After a week of having my first dose of chemotherapy I started feeling a weird pain in my hair. How is it possible is to feel pain in your hair? Whenever I washed my hair or brushed it I felt pain right at the hair follicles. It was not a headache; it was "hair-ache." Seriously! I had to wash my head in slow motion and brush my hair gently. Even the wind bothered me.

One day, I'm telling Angel about my "hair pain" and he decided to give me a hair massage. Bad decision! I howled like a hurt puppy and he jumped up in surprise repeating, "What did I do? What happened? I didn't do anything!" My kids came running to our room, they were alarmed and asking, "What happened? What happened?" It was quite an event. I had to calm everybody down, including myself. So learn from my mistake. Do not ever attempt any hair massages!

The day came for my second session of chemotherapy. I told my doctor about the "hair-ache" and about the crazy incident of the hair massage idea while laughing at the whole situation. She told me that that was a sign that I would soon be losing my hair. Within approximately 72 hours of my second session, it happened.

It's Happening!

I was taking a shower and suddenly I saw a bunch of hair on the floor. My heart jumped and I gasped in astonishment. I thought, "Okay, it's happening." I looked at my arms and body. I was all covered with hair! It was so much hair, that I started moving all the hair away from the drain with my foot to avoid clogging the drain. I touched my head and looked at my hand; my hand was full of hair. I was a hairy mess!

"Calm down . . . calm down . . ." I repeated to myself. "All is well."

I stepped out the shower and grabbed a towel to try to take the hair off my face. I slowly dried my hair, or what was left of it, to try to remove as much hair as I could. The towel then became a hairy mess. A look in the mirror revealed bald patches on my head.

I put the towel aside and started pulling strands of my hair to see if I could remove it by hand. To my surprise, I could do it easily without any pain. It was as if my hair didn't have any roots at all. Some was coming out easily by just grabbing it without even pulling. There were yet some hair patches that it was still painful to pull. I was shocked, but calm.

After cleaning up the hairy mess I left in the bathroom I put on a headscarf and went downstairs. Angel was busy making a snack for the kids in the kitchen. I approached him and whispered in his ear:

"Papa. It's happening," I said while pointing to my head.

He clearly knew what I was talking about. He smiled at me, then he hugged me.

"Are you okay?" he asked.

"Yeah, I'm okay. I'm calm. But I just want to pull it all out at once and I can't," I replied.

I told him what happened while I was taking a shower. We went upstairs and I showed him the hair in the trash can. I showed him the bald spots on my head and how I was trying to get the rest of my hair out.

"Do you want me to shave your head?" he asked me.

"Yes. Let's do it. I want to go through with this at once," I said.

Angel tried using the hair clipper on my head to remove the remaining hair, but there were still a few spots too painful to shave. I still had "bald spots" of pure scalp showing so he suggested that he try to remove the remaining hair with a razor. I was already feeling tired and told him to continue in the family room while we watched TV.

I knew that the kids were watching TV in the family room. Since I was upstairs I asked the kids in a loud voice to pick a movie for all of us to watch. I put my headscarf back on and went downstairs. While approaching the family room, I could listen to them trying to decide which movie to watch. When I got there I smiled and asked:

"Do you like my headscarf?"

"Already?" Alejandro asked knowing what I was referring to.

"Almost," I replied.

"Mama, you look pretty!" Gabriel said.

I then received kisses by the dozen. I told them that we were going to enjoy a movie together while dad was going to help me shave the rest of my head. We started the movie and Angel came to the room with a nice and warm towel and put it on my head. "This should open the follicles so that it doesn't hurt," he said.

He was very gentle while shaving my head. It was like being at a spa. The kids occasionally looked at me while watching the movie and threw flying kisses at me. Sometimes they stared a little bit and smiled at me. I gave them a wink and smiled back at them. I don't even remember what movie we saw that afternoon, but I do remember the many times I heard their beautiful encouraging voices say, "I love you mama."

Finally, Angel said, "Done!" and kissed my head. "Nice! It's very soft!" he added. "Go ahead! Touch it!" he told me. I touched my head and smiled. Wow! It was really soft.

"Can I touch? Can I touch?" the kids asked while rushing to me.

"Yeah, go ahead!" I told them.

"So soft!" they exclaimed while gently touching my head.

"Who want to kiss me on the head?" I asked.

Immediately, a bunch of kisses decorated my freshly shaven head.

> ***Journal Entry***
>
> No more hair brushing, hair styling, nor bad hair days for a while! Welcome hats, scarves, wigs, wind and sun!

Don't Think About What's Missing

For various days afterwards I shopped for scarves and hats. I didn't feel comfortable wearing a wig. I wore it a couple of times, but for some reason I didn't feel I "fit" with it.

I decided to put away anything that reminded me that once I had hair. I stored in boxes all my hair related products and accessories. I didn't want anything to remind me I was missing something. That way, I could focus on "sailing with the wind" instead of fighting it and on how I wanted to project myself. I remembered the saying, "Bald is beautiful." Yes, it is indeed.

Unbelievable Moments

A week after the second chemo session, I was feeling good, full of energy. I decided to go to work. I put on a headscarf, a hat, smiled at myself in the mirror and drove to work. My friend Kat, gave me a big hug when she saw me and complimented me on how beautiful I was.

"So, it finally came off?" she asked me.

"Yeah. Completely."

"Can I see?" she asked again.

I hesitated for a brief moment, before I took off my hat and scarf. "What do I have to hide?" I thought. "Oh Yilda, you are beautiful!" she replied before giving me another hug.

Kat had been giving me a lot of support. Her father died from cancer and her mother was a breast cancer survivor. She told me she was going to shave her head. I told her that she didn't have to do that. She had previously told me that if I had to go through chemo she would shave her hair for me in support, just as she had done for her dad. It didn't matter what I said or how I tried to persuade her. She grabbed me by the hand and said, "C'mon girl shut up. I'm, going to do it. We are going to be two beautiful bald heads in the office—wait, we are really going to be three because Mike's already bald." Mike was one of the other engineers in our work group.

What followed was a very moving experience. My co-workers showed up in my office welcoming me and expressing a lot of concern for me. The girls in the office got together and went with Kat and I to the barbershop. Once Kat sat on the chair at the barbershop we all made a circle. I was Kat's side as we held each others' hands and prayed.

The barber, Rudy, began to shave Kat's head. Layer by layer her hair was falling to the floor and with each layer my tears of joy and love were silently flowing. A lot of co-workers from other sections also showed up in the barbershop sharing hugs and words of encouragement. A loving crowd overflowed the small barbershop. I watched all that was happening and I was in disbelief. I was becoming aware of the family I had at work. God was surrounding me with love. It was a wonderful experience to feel and share the love and all the good wishes of so many people. I had nothing to hide, not even my beautiful and shiny bald head.

As soon as the barber finished shaving Kat's hair I took off my headscarf and kissed her head. There were many tears, hugs and kisses. Love was overflowing in everyone there. We walked out the place showing our shiny heads through the corridors on our way back to the office. We came across Mike in the hallway and he looked at us in surprise. He stopped to give us a hug. The three of us then walked together to the office. Once there, we took a picture of us smiling and happily showing our heads. I felt liberated.

As soon as the barber finished shaving Kat's hair I took off my headscarf and kissed her head.

That day I received many small gifts . . . commemorative breast cancer pins, caps, earrings and cards. One of the police officers, who worked in a different floor, showed up in our work space and took off his hat to show us that he, too, had shaved his head. He had heard the news and wanted to show his support.

It had been a while since I had written to my friends in Puerto Rico to give them an update. After that incredible day at the office I had to share that wonderful experience. I was still almost speechless. Here is part of the message I sent to my friends:

"Hi there! It has been a while. I'm going through chemo and recovering just on time for my next session. I'm working intermittently as the treatment and recovery allow me. Every time I see God's hand working in my family and me I feel strong. I have had ups and downs, but it is amazing how God is always present.

By the way, I already lost my hair. Therefore, everything feels breezy on top of my head. I'm not yet used to the wig, so my fashion now is using headscarves and hats. The good thing is that for a while I don't have to fight no more with "bad hair" days, nor with tangles or untangling. Oh, and it feels very nice when the kids kiss me on the head.

I have to tell you about a very special day I had at work. A friend of mine, Kat, decided to shave her head in support. It was a very moving moment. Everyone there was sharing tears and hugs. Love filled the place. Many approached to me offering to donate me leave hours to help me in case I needed it to remain in pay status. I talked to people I knew and to others I didn't know. Then my friend and I walked through the corridors with our beautiful shiny heads with joy and the rest of the group behind us. It was very touching and fun at the same time. It was like a liberating experience. I don't know how to explain it. Later that day one of the police officers showed up in my space with his head shaved to show his support.

Please, I don't expect you to start shaving your heads. Oh no! I already know that I have your love, your support and your prayers. I only tell this to you so that you know that God has surrounded me with so many beautiful people and that I am not alone.

I don't know how more to thank the Lord. I only hope that the Lord shows me each day how to share the blessings and the love He gives me."

After I sent that message I received a lot of encouragement and words of love. I filled with joy. One of the notes I received that really touched me during those days was from a friend who told me, "What you are living is reaching others and touching many. Thank you for sharing your life and hope with us." Those words inspired me. This was not happening for nothing. I had a mission. I had to keep fighting the good battle of faith.

You thrill me, Lord, with all you have done for me!
I sing for joy because of what you have done.
(Psalms 92:4, NLT)

Just Fooling Around

When I went shopping for wigs I chose one with a different color from my previous black hair. The people who didn't know me would have never realized I was wearing a wig. A few times I wore it so I could play being "in disguise" just for fun. I had never used the wig to my medical appointments and one day I decided to wear it just to see what would happen.

When I opened the door Dorothy was at the front desk—with a kind smile as always. She had to look at me twice to recognize me. As I was talking to her one of the nurses, Amber, stopped by the front desk to talk to Dorothy. Dorothy told her to meet "the new patient," pointing to me. When Amber saw me, I said "Hi Amber!" She was amazed. "I love the color!" she said. Without using words, she indicated to me we should keep it a secret to see the reaction of the staff.

It was not until I entered the clinic to have my vitals taken that I saw Elizabeth. The same previous reaction was repeated again and again as I came accross with the rest of the staff. Between hugs after the immediate excitement, I told everybody not to tell Dr. Kazhdan. After the brief moment of excitement and laughter, everyone was immediately saying, "Shhhhh. Let's keep it down . . . the doctor is around."

I could sense that Dr. Kazhdan was approaching. I saw her when she stopped at the far end of the corridor to talk to one of the nurses. She looked at me from the distance, probably thinking maybe I was a new patient. When I looked at her right into the eyes and greeted her, she approached me with her always characteristic beautiful big smile and gave me a big hug. "Mrs Rivera! You look so different!" Dr. Kazhdan said in astonishment.

The nurses and technicians were all laughing, and they kept introducing me to her as if I was a new patient. I had a great time with my look that day. It's great always to share a few good laughs, especially with people that want the best for you. I was so glad I found them. Thanks to God for that wonderful healthcare team!

> *Journal Entry*
>
> Thanks to my wonderful healthcare team! Thanks to my wonderful family! This cancer experience sucks less because of you all.

Even in my work place I had fun with the wig. Once I introduced myself to my supervisor telling him that I was a new engineer and that someone had told me that he was the boss. He nearly burst laughing. That day I was the "new engineer" in the office.

> *Journal Entry*
>
> Yesterday, while studying with kids I had a hot flash, one of those caused by chemo. My faced turned all red and I felt like I was burning inside. I immediately removed my headscarf to feel better and fresh, and told them: "See? If I had hair I couldn't do this. That's one of the benefits of baldness." We all share a big laugh.

No Eyebrows, No Eyelashes

A few weeks after I lost my hair I started losing my eyebrows, then my eyelashes. I looked pale. The good thing was I didn't have to shave my legs for a long time. This was a nice perk.

In spite of my appearance, I didn't want people to have pity for me or see me as a "sick person." Therefore I proudly wore my headscarf, put on some eyeliner and walked with my chin up. If people looked or stared at me, I smiled back at them. I wanted people to see me as a warrior.

> **Journal Entry**
>
> No hair, no eyebrows, no eyelashes . . . but feeling a blessed breeze of energy. I want to swim, run, live, laugh and love! I'm gonna drive Angel crazy today.

A Source of Inspiration

God was truly blessing me through a wonderful support chain. Friends, family and other people were praying constantly and sending positive thoughts. I still read their messages and they still inspire me.

One Fine Day

One day we made doing the laundry chore an improvised game and a family activity. Angel came to the master bedroom with a big pile of clean clothes and dumped them on the floor to sort. I was on the bed with a few painkillers in me. The kids were also on the bed with me watching TV. Angel was taking on his shoulders a big part of the household chores. He was doing the laundry, the dishes, the cooking. He was being strong, but I knew he was tired. He sat on the floor in the middle of the pile of clothes sorting out every piece and doing individual stacks. It was a way for him to complete this tedious but important chore and at the same time to be with us in the bedroom. I decided to get out of bed, in spite of the painkillers, and sit with him on the floor and help him sort. That was something I could do . . . and it made me happy to be able to help. I also called the kids to help us out. We all moved to the floor. We started with this "whose is this?" game with the kids to separate the garments by owner. Angel and I looked at each other and smiled . . . it was working.

The kids brought the hangers. They were moving back and forth filling the closets and drawers with clean clothes. We thanked the kids in the process. We let them know they were greatly helping mom and dad, and that they were doing something important . . . very important. We told them that by helping with the housework, they were increasing the quality time to spend with mom and dad. They liked the idea and continued helping until all the clothes were in their corresponding place. They felt important knowing that what they were doing was something valuable. They felt like they were making a difference. In fact, they really were.

We finished in no time. We had all enjoyed a simple and tedious chore together. Soon enough, we were all laying in the bed like lizards and watching TV.

A Source of Inspiration

Psalm 23, a New Meaning

I started to read this Psalm every night to my kids so they could memorize it. We even discussed it verse by verse. I wanted them to understand the meaning of each line to hold onto our Lord if they felt any fear. I told them that to feel fear is normal, but that we had to put faith in front of it. I wanted to give them the tools to help them grow and to prepare them for life. Faith vs. fear is a constant battle. I told my kids, "If fear appears at your door you have two options, either you choose to let it in or you choose to grab onto the Lord and the promise of His presence no matter what." I felt an urgency to share this with them; I had no time to lose.

> *If fear appears at your door you have two options, either you choose to let it in or you choose to grab onto the Lord and the promise of His presence no matter what.*

Like a revelation, at some point that Psalm took on a new meaning for me. I read it in different versions, both in Spanish and in English. One day while I was reading the New Century Version:

> *The LORD is my shepherd;*
> *I have everything I need.*

That second phrase got into me. "I have everything I need, I shall not want, I lack nothing"—I thought. Then I kept reading and stopped at verse 4.

> *² He lets me rest in green pastures.*
> *He leads me to calm water.*
> *³ He gives me new strength.*
> *He leads me on paths that are right*
> *for the good of his name.*
> *⁴ Even if I walk through a very dark valley,*
> *I will not be afraid,*
> *because you are with me.*
> *Your rod and your shepherd's staff comfort me.*

I meditated for a while. Then, I had this thought, "I know that God has already healed me . . . but I still need to go through this path because God wants to show me something."

So I prayed:

"Lord, put in my heart the words you want me to write and the words you want me to say. May your Holy Spirit dwell in me so that you guide my words and my thoughts. All I am is yours."

Conversations with Kids

I tried to be conscious at every moment to give the boys living testimony of our God's grace so that they could experience in their own lives God's promises and God's presence. Sometimes we spoke about cancer because they had questions. Cancer was just something there, in the way, but our Lord's presence was certain, with us and in us, and much more powerful.

I wanted my little ones to understand the concept that God is in control and that He is with us. Healing is one of the things that our Lord can do, of course, but I wanted my boys to experience and witness that God's grace and His power were with us in the middle of the storm and that He was helping all of us to get through this together.

One day, I was watching TV with Gabriel. We were not talking; just leaning toward each other watching a TV program. He suddenly asked me out of the blue:

"Mom, what's that thing's name . . .?"—he made a pause as if he was trying to remember something—"ah, that thing . . . the breast cancer," he added. "How . . .? How that thing got into you? Why is that happening to you?" my little Gabriel lovingly asked me with concern, when I was going through chemotherapy.

"You know . . . I don't know. Nobody knows exactly why or how. All I know it's not anybody's fault. It's a mystery. The doctors don't even know. But I do know that God is with us and he takes care of us, and that He will show us His wonderful grace and His presence if we ask Him," I replied with a hug.

I wanted him to understand that no matter how things look or seem to be, God has something wonderful for us. After a pause he smiled at me and hugged me back and kissed me:

"I love you mom."

A Source of Inspiration

"I love you more," I replied.

'Nah, I love you more!" he replied with a mischievous playful smile.

"Naaaahh . . . I love you more," I replied back tickling him.

"No. I love you more, more, more, more . . .!"—he was laughing with each "more" while squeezing me with hugs.

"Okay! Okay! You won. I give up!"

We hugged each other. After a while, he fell asleep in my arms. Soon after, I also fell asleep. The picture on the next page is a reminder of that moment. I wish it was better quality, but my husband took it with a cell phone and in low light.

Every time I look at it, it reminds me to look at my blessings . . . to look at the masterpiece, the melody, the symphony that God is orchestrating in me. God guards us in His peace that goes beyond all understanding. In Him, we rest.

Every time I look at the picture, it reminds me to look at my blessings. It reminds me to look at the masterpiece, the melody, the symphony that God is orchestrating in me. God guards us in His peace that goes beyond all understanding. In Him, we rest.

Cool? Really?

One day Alejandro helped vacuum the house. It was beautiful to watch him! While he was vacuuming he told me, "Hey mom, this is not so difficult . . . it feels cool!"

Then I think he reconsidered what he had just said and clarified, "Of course . . . it is not as if one would like to do this every day."

Remembering

My kids have grown up so much. I'm speechless on the way they express their thoughts and their love. Today Alejandro kissed Gabriel and hugged him while he was crying, because he didn't want to get a bath.

COURAGE UNDER FIRE

"Mom . . . Why is that happening to you?" . . . We hugged each other. After a while, he fell asleep in my arms.

A Source of Inspiration

Remembering

Potty Time

I remember when Gabriel started to do his potty in the toilet. He chased me telling me, "Mom, potty," for me to get him to the bathroom. One day before his afternoon nap I put him a diaper to make sure there were no "accidents." When he was almost asleep, I slowly left the bedroom and closed the door carefully without making a sound. As soon as I closed the door, I heard, "Mom, potty." I waited. He repeated, "Mooomy, poootty." I left for about 10 minutes thinking that he was looking for an excuse to escape from naptime. After the 10-minute trial period, I came back to his room and put my ear to the door. I heard him playing in his bed. I slowly opened the door and saw this little boy's angry face looking at me firmly, "Mom! I did my potty"—while pointing to his diaper. What a little boy!

Later that same day, the kids were playing in my bed while I was trying to get a nap. I was trying to "hide" and get some quiet time because Angel was on travel. I asked the boys to play in their room to give me a little bit of time to rest so they went to Alejandro's room. I followed them and out of the blue, I suggested Alejandro to read a short story book to Gabriel—at that time Alejandro didn't yet know how to read. He took that seriously and grabbed a book, "A Boy Wants a Dinosaur"[1]—one of Alejandro's favorite books at that time. They both sat in the bed and I left and closed the door, but decided to stay at the door to hear what they were going to do. To my surprise, Alejandro started "reading" the book. He had memorized the story! It was an immense feeling!

Thrilled, I started walking to my room when their bedroom door opened behind me. It was Alejandro running toward me in excitement.

"Mom, mom! I know how to read this book! Sit there, let me show you." He sat by my side and started "reading" it to me.

In the meanwhile I heard a little voice approaching, "Mom! Potty!"

Journal Entry

I'm feeling better and with more energy. I took a walk with the kids and the dog around the neighborhood. I had a great time with them. Gabriel was staying behind sometimes with this "I'm tired face." At some point he questioned me with whining eyes why we walked. I said that walking was going to help me recover better. So he replied, "Oh! That's good!"—and he speeded up to pick up our pace. He found his own motivation.

Journal Entry

The first words I heard this morning, "mama"—and then a sleepy hug. Mmmm.

2011 Susan G. Komen Race for the Cure, San Juan, PR

This was an awesome moment. It is still difficult to find the words to describe it. A couple of friends and family members decided to walk in my honor during this event. I was thrilled looking at all the pictures my friends and family sent me as they walked. Doraima, my sister, also called me and texted me from time to time telling me where they were at different moments during the walk.

My friends, Ana Luz, Heloisa and Blanca, made a big sign with my picture and name on it. Thanks to that sign, Doraima was able to find them and they continued walking together. I started receiving messages from people who didn't know I was going through cancer who had become aware because of the sign. They started sending me messages that they were walking for someone else and that now they also had me in their thoughts and prayers.

It was so amazing and very moving. My friend Blanca texted me that she found Doraima and my parents. At the same time I received a message from Doraima that she saw a sign with my picture and found Blanca's group. After a while I received a message from my sister telling me that someone who knew me approached them sending me greetings and "get well" wishes.

A Source of Inspiration

In every picture I saw that big sign moving all the way with them. It was as if I were walking with them. (Sign reads, "In Honor of Yilda, keep fighting")

My friends and my sister sent picture after picture to my cell phone and to my e-mail. In every picture I saw that big sign moving all the way with them. It was as if I were walking with them. All that was very encouraging. I spent most of that day by the computer and with my cell phone in my hands, just to keep up with all the pictures they were posting. With those pictures, I made an album. I wanted to remember that moment as it happened.

Friends, Prayers and Family

The "Susan G. Komen Walk for the Cure" in PR was such as moving day. I was humbled and thrilled with joy and tears of amazement. I was so moved by my sister's constant updates and pictures while she was walking and by the pictures that other friends were sending to me.

It was inspiring the amount of encouraging words I received later on about other people having me in their thoughts while walking or running in the Susan G. Komen event in other places. They sent me pictures, as well, in support. Loving notes from my parents, my other sisters and relatives overfilled my heart.

Sometime later one very special friend that I hadn't seen in a long time, Istra, called me to tell me she was doing the "Olympic Triathlon 5150" in Galveston, TX. She wanted my approval to use my name associated with the breast cancer fight in the event. Wow! It was not only a great joy to hear her again, but also awesome and breathtaking to know that someone would be representing me and the breast cancer fight for the cure in such an event. Again, wow!

Many times, Angel's strength and the prayers and messages of many other people were all that kept me afloat. Although many times I couldn't go to church, I knew that there were people praying for me there, in other countries and in other churches and groups. I could feel all their prayers. One of my friends, Zory, sent me a pink prayer-shawl, hand-knitted while in prayer. That was an amazing gift! I wore it often around the house and it brough me joy and strength.

I was surrounded with so much love that I didn't have enough words to thank everyone. The many words of encouragement received and special visits all reminded me of how blessed I was and inspired me to "keep up the good fight."

A Source of Inspiration

> ### *Journal Entry*
>
> One of my friends is coming to see me and to be with me for a while because Angel is traveling. I really appreciate that gesture, even more knowing that she decided to leave her little baby girl and boys to be with me for a couple of days. That is really valuable to me.

> ### *Journal Entry*
>
> THANKS Blanca for the magic of your visit. One of the best moments: The memory of how HAPPY I was when I saw that yellow cab approaching. Wow! Thanks for the gift of that memory.

You thrill me, Lord, with all you have done for me!
I sing for joy because of what you have done.
(Psalms 92:4, NLT)

Coping with Neutropenia

A potential side effect to watch for while undergoing chemotherapy is neutropenia. Neutropenia is a disorder characterized by an abnormally low number of neutrophils, the most important type of white blood cell (WBC). The neutrophils are produced in the bone marrow and help the immune system fight off infections. They make up approximately 50 to 70 percent of all WBC. The lower your neutrophil count, the more vulnerable you are to infections. If you have severe neutropenia, the bacteria normally present in your mouth and digestive tract can cause infections. Therefore, patients with neutropenia are more susceptible to bacterial infections and without prompt medical attention, the condition may become life-threatening. Little did I know that neutropenia was going to have a huge impact on my treatment.

No Mouth Kissing!

A couple of days after my first treatment, it hit me very hard. Various readings of my WBC count were so low that they were not even showing on my lab results. I was told I had severe neutropenia and that it was a very delicate and serious situation. Nurse Elizabeth was very serious and briefed me thoroughly about all the precautions I should take for the next few days until my neutrophils count improved. Angel was with me that day and Elizabeth also explained the precautions to him. On several occasions she reiterated how delicate and serious the situation was, as to ensure that both of us take whatever steps were necessary to avoid jeopardizing my health.

While briefing me on the "DOs and DON'Ts," Elizabeth paused and asked me if I had any pets. I told her we had a dog. Immediately she emphasized to stay away from the dog and avoid petting it.

I guess Angel felt the need to add some humor to the grim situation and said, "Huh! Yilda you heard that? No more mouth kisses to the doggy!"

Elizabeth looked at me in astonishment and disbelief and said, "Yilda!"

"That's a lie!" I replied to Elizabeth while looking at Angel in disbelief for what he had just said. "I never do that . . .! Angel!"

Elizabeth realized that Angel was just fooling around and we laughed. Then she continued talking to make us very aware of the safety and health precautions to take around the house for the next few days to minimize any potential risk of infection. Before leaving the clinic, I was given a medication to stimulate the growth of white blood cells in my body. I had to take that medication for the next few days and my blood was going to be monitored closely to see if my immune system was responding.

When we were getting ready to leave, Elizabeth gave both of us a big kiss and hug. As we approached the door, she said in a loud voice,

"Oh! And Mrs. Rivera . . . no more mouth kissing the dog!"

Amber was getting into the room when she heard that and stopped to say: "What?!"—and made an "Eww" face.

"That's not true! I don't do that!" I looked at both Elizabeth and Amber, now in disbelief and giving the wide-open eyes look to Elizabeth.

We all laughed. Elizabeth approached and said to Angel with a very serious look on her face, "You, take good care of her!"

"I will. Of course I will do so. I always do." Angel replied firmly while thanking her for caring so much for me.

Then she gave us another hug and said, "Everything will be okay. Just follow the rules and call us if you have questions, feel dehydrated or anything happens."

Neutropenia and Medication Side Effects

I had to deal also with the associated side effects of the medication to help boost my neutrophils count, the most bothersome of which were bone pain and muscle aches. I had to cope not only with the constant pain caused by the medication and the sides effects of the chemo, but also with the isolation during those four to five days that I was severely neutropenic, immediately after my regular dose of chemo.

I had to be separated in a room away from my kids. That was painful. I was basically defenseless even against my own body. The kids blew flying kisses to me from the doorway and we played blowing and catching kisses with each other. Hands-washing for everyone entering the room was a must. Angel and I had to learn how to handle my restrictive diet and routine when I was neutropenic.

Coping with neutropenia was cumbersome. At some point during the treatment I developed an infection. I knew I was in deep trouble when I saw Dr. Kazhdan's face when she told me that I had an infection and that I was severely neutropenic at the same time. She called Elizabeth to the room. I knew I was in very deep trouble when my oncologist called another doctor to see me immediately to discuss the treatment and coordinate the treatment plan along with the chemotherapy. If I didn't respond to the treatment, the chemotherapy would have to be postponed and that was not good at all.

Chemotherapy is administered in cycles. These vary depending on the type of chemo you are receiving. Cycles could be altered depending on how you react to the chemo but there is not much flexibility without compromising the effectiveness of the whole treatment. I felt like I was immersed in a deep dark cloud.

I was immensely worried. I was sad. I just waited. I also prayed a lot. I worshiped the Lord of my life and put my worries and woes before Him.

> [5] *Why, my soul, are you downcast? Why so disturbed within*
> *me? Put your hope in God, for I will yet praise him,*
> *my Savior and my God.*
> *(Psalms 42:5, NIV)*

> *Though an army besiege me, my heart will not fear;*
> *though war break out against me,*
> *even then I will be confident.*
> *(Psalms 27:3, NIV)*

Thanks to God, I started responding to both the neutropenia medication and the antibiotics and we didn't have to delay the chemotherapy for long. The doctors didn't want to declare victory yet; however, they watched me closely for the next couple of weeks. I was not off the hook by any means.

Something Bigger

As chemotherapy was cyclic, the neutropenia was cyclic as well. I could expect to get severely neutropenic near the fifth day after the chemo dose. All of us knew the drill and prepared for it. Many times I told Angel to take the kids to an outdoor activity and have fun while I stayed home. I didn't want them to sacrifice their ability to go out, relax and have a good time away from home.

In the meantime, I had to stay away from crowded places to avoid being exposed to germs or bacteria as my body was defenseless to fight them. I couldn't help but be filled with sadness during those days I was neutropenic. Since I couldn't go to church, I visited my church's web site to hear the sermons.

One of those sermons was about 2 Corinthians 1. It was food for my soul. I was touched immediately by the first part of this chapter that explains how the Lord comforts us in all our troubles so that we can comfort others in trouble with the comfort we ourselves have received from God (verse 4). Verse 5 adds that in the same way the sufferings of Christ flow into our lives, so also through Christ our comfort overflows. When reading this, I declared that the power of my Lord was overflowing in me. It restored me and fed my soul.

God is wonderful through His Word. He is faithful to His Word.

> [20] *For no matter how many promises God has made, they are "Yes" in Christ. And so through him the "Amen" is spoken by us to the glory of God.* [21] *Now it is God who makes both us and you stand firm in Christ. He anointed us,* [22] *set his seal of ownership on us, and put his Spirit in our hearts as a deposit, guaranteeing what is to come.*
> *(2 Corinthians 1:20-22, NIV)*

In the midst of difficult circumstances God's grace is manifested. I was then a vase of clay ready to receive the best wine. I was a beaten body to receive the lifting and healing power of the Lord. I repeated in my mind, "He is in control. My worries and woes are before Him. He cares for me and he knows my prayer before I even come before His presence. He will provide." Many times I didn't have words to pray. I just stood there in silence and in awe longing to stay in His presence.

> *In the same way, the Spirit helps us in our weakness. We do not know what we ought to pray for, but the Spirit himself intercedes for us through wordless groans.*
> *(Romans 8:26, NIV)*

> [15] *For you did not receive a spirit that makes you a slave again to fear, but you received the Spirit of sonship. And by him we cry, "Abba, Father." [16] The Spirit himself testifies with our spirit that we are God's children.*
> [17] *Now if we are children, then we are heirs—heirs of God and co-heirs with Christ, if indeed we share in his sufferings in order that we may also share in his glory.*
> [18] *I consider that our present sufferings are not worth comparing with the glory that will be revealed in us.*
> *(Romans 8:15-18, NKJV)*

At some point in my quiet time with the Lord, I came to the understanding that all that was happening to me was not about *me*. I had to pray. I had to pray for my children, for my husband, for my family, for my doctors and nurses, for my friends and for all who I come in contact with. "This is not about me; there is something bigger in all this," I thought.

> *And pray in the Spirit on all occasions with all kinds of prayers and requests. With this in mind, be alert and always keep on praying for all the Lord's people.*
> *(Ephesians 6:18, NIV)*

> [8] *"For my thoughts are not your thoughts, neither are your ways my ways," declares the Lord. [9] "As the heavens are higher than the earth, so are my ways higher than your ways and my thoughts than your thoughts.*
> *(Isaiah 55:8-9, NIV)*

I didn't question the peace that was filling me over and over, because I knew where it came from.

> [6] *Do not be anxious about anything, but in every situation, by prayer and petition, with thanksgiving, present your requests to God. [7] And the peace of God, which transcends all understanding, will guard your hearts and your minds in Christ Jesus.*
> *(Philippians 4:6-7, NIV)*

> **Journal Entry**
>
> I'm again with severe neutropenia, so no chemotherapy today. Every time chemo is cancelled, it is not good news. That means that my body didn't recover as expected.
>
> *He will cover you with his feathers, and under his wings you can hide.*
> *His truth will be your shield and protection.*
> (Psalms 91:4, NCV)

Somber Days

My second chemotherapy regime had to change because I had a very adverse reaction to Taxol. Taxol is an anti-cancer chemotherapy drug. I developed an acute peripheral neuropathy[1] at the very beginning of the Taxol administration. That was unexpected and very unusual. That was not supposed to happen. Peripheral neuropathy is more common at a low degree at the end of that treatment characterized by the feeling of numbness in the finger and toes, or the sensation of pins and needles, but in my

> *I didn't question the peace that was filling me over and over, because I knew where it came from.*

case, the peripheral neuropathy was so acute that I had a feeling of "burning" or being "eaten by fire ants" if my hands had any friction with something and if I was standing or walking for a brief amount of time. I couldn't even hold the steering wheel with my hands without feeling pain. I couldn't dress without feeling pain because of the friction between my hands and the fabric. I could feel that burning-like sensation behind my neck with sun exposure. I immediately had to see a neurologist to determine the extent of the nerve damage and the treatment. In the chapter about "Coping with the Leftovers" I will speak about this a bit more.

With Taxol I didn't suffer from severe neutropenia, but because I couldn't tolerate it, my doctor decided to replace the Taxol regime with CMF, which is a combination of three chemotherapy drugs: Cyclophosphamide, Methotrexate and 5 Fluorouracil. This meant that the projected statistics to reduce the cancer recurrence with the particular adjuvant chemotherapy I had been receiving no longer applied to me. Another door to the unknown had been opened. The doctor told me that my body would let her know how many cycles were going to be necessary.

One day I felt good and strong. I felt happy because I was able to tolerate the new chemo regime, or so I thought. After my latest blood test the doctor told me that they were going to have to stop the chemo because my body couldn't take it anymore. I was shocked. Although I felt good the neutrophils count decreased once again. Although I did not have severe neutropenia, I was still at high risk and my neutrophils count was still decreasing.

The doctor told me that my bone marrow was "speaking" to us; it was exhausted of fighting the effects of the chemo. I had to have more injections than usual and thus more pain, for a few more days to help my bone marrow produce WBCs and increase the neutrophils count. Also, I had to stop taking Cyclophosphamide. I was going to have one more infusion in the next few days to ensure my body recovered sufficiently to finish the second cycle of that chemo regime. After that I was going to be done with chemo. Once we completed the imaging screening and verified the results we were going to discuss the possibility of radiation therapy and further hormonal therapy.

> *Journal Entry*
>
> I'll be staying at home tomorrow; my health is first. Sometimes I worry if I would have enough leave left to cover for my testing, treatment and medical appointments. As soon as this worry looms, the "God is taking care of me" inner voice comes and rescues me. Yes, God is taking care of me.

Every time I was hit with severe neutropenia, I couldn't help but get sad. On one of those days I felt I needed to write something. I strongly held the pen in my hand and grabbed my journal. I started to remember happy moments with my husband and kids. So many memories brought me happiness. Then I put pen to paper and wrote the following words:

> ### *Journal Entry*
>
> #### If I Ever Leave This World
>
> I look at you, and I thank the Lord for the opportunity He gave me to be your mother. If I ever leave this world, I would leave happy; with joy in my heart because of the opportunity I had to love you, to guide you, to teach you, to show you all things I know, to guide you in Math (my favorite subject) and to witness how smart you are getting every day.
>
> I would leave happy to have known a husband to be by my side, fighting together with me. I would leave happy because you value and prioritize the time with us, your family. I would leave with joy for your love and to be able to love God together with you.

The neutropenia was now interrupting my treatment. There I was, with an unfinished chemotherapy treatment at the mercy of a cancer that threatened my life. Then like a thunder the Word of God took me away from that thought. The Casting Crowns song "Voice of Truth" had been in my mind all afternoon after I left the doctor's office. The Word of God was telling me not to be afraid. It was telling me to lean on Him, to depend on Him. My Lord was reminding me to keep my trust in Him. So I prayed:

"Every step I take, O Lord, I give it to you. I will choose to listen and trust your Word. Your Word is truth."

After I prayed I realized I hadn't checked the daily Bible verse I received in my e-mail every day. I opened it and this was the verse waiting to be read, in my inbox, at the time I needed it the most:

> [3] *You, Lord, give true peace to those who depend on you,*
> *because they trust you.* [4] *So, trust the Lord always,*
> *because he is our Rock forever.*
> *(Isaiah 26:3-4, NCV)*

I wanted to praise the Lord so badly I couldn't even find the words. Then I went into my bed and rested. A good peaceful rest was very important for my body to recover. I slept with this verse in my mind:

COURAGE UNDER FIRE

*Now faith is confidence in what we hope for
and assurance about what we do not see.
(Hebrews 11:1, NIV)*

Journal Entry

Here I am . . . in Your hands, in Your hands marked by love.

Coping with Exhaustion

More Than a Physical State

Exhaustion goes beyond being just a physical side effect of chemotherapy or radiation. In my case, I also had to learn how to fight emotional and mental exhaustion. I had to learn to acknowledge that exhaustion to be able to fight it. In that way, I could make the conscious choice to crawl if I couldn't walk, and to breathe slowly if I felt like I wasn't breathing.

Often I had to mentally rest and focus on something bigger than my own situation to be able to recharge my batteries, to keep moving on and fighting. One day, I was just getting through the day minute-by-minute. I was extremely tired. I was taking one step after another asking the Lord to renew my strength to get through the day. All my worries and my own situation were a heavy load on my shoulders and in my mind.

I was in a deep silence most of that day, trying to focus my mind on projects at work and putting a great deal of effort toward putting my personal situation aside. By noon, I was emotionally and mentally exhausted. An extreme tiredness was even suffocating my thoughts. I was having lunch with my friend Todd in the cafeteria. At some point I opened my mouth to say:

"I feel so exhausted . . ." I said and took a deep breath. "Today is one of those days I'm just waiting to get through it and be over with it. I'm exhausted and I don't know why . . ."

At that moment my strength and composure betrayed me. I burst into tears. A river of slow and silent tears started flowing and flowing. I couldn't contain them. I only had the strength to put my face in my hands and breathe . . . breathe slowly. At that time, I hadn't yet started the chemotherapy and I was already feeling so worn out. Saying that I didn't know why I was feeling so exhausted made me depressed, but I didn't want to be sad. I didn't want to be worried.

I think I was entering to a huge, foggy cloud of uncertainty. Worries about my kids, my family, the situation being out of my hands; it was a tough load. Maybe it was uncertainty. Maybe it was the emotional distress of the constant decision making in a short time frame. Maybe it was the fact of my extended family and many close friends being an ocean away from me. I can't point to a single reason, but only say that I felt physically, emotionally and mentally spent.

Todd offered me to take a walk outside if I could. He didn't ask me anything. We just walked in silence. At some point he put his hand in my shoulder. I knew he was praying for me in silence. For me it was a long walk . . . I didn't know if I was going to make it back to the office.

An unknown pain and agony was overwhelming and choking me. "One step after the other... one at a time." I reminded myself. My only prayer at that moment was:

"Oh God, renew my face, renew my strength, renew my spirit, renew my faith. Help me take one step at a time."

> ### Journal Entry
>
> I see Gabriel growing up and then I remember when he was younger. He was so little he couldn't reach the lavatory faucets in the bathroom. He used a toothbrush as a tool to open and close the faucets. I was impressed by that small detail and I thought: "He is growing up and learning to solve his own situations." He couldn't add height to his stature, but he didn't give up.
>
> Then I thought that if he chose to manage the obstacles to be able to reach, I was going to choose to reach out to the Lord and not to give up.

"Be Still"

One Sunday at church we sang the song "Still" from Hillsong United. With every verse, I was singing my life; I was singing my journey. Every time I was feeling exhausted, I played that song and meditated on the lyrics. I invite you to look and to listen that song. It reminded me of Psalm 46.

> [1] *God is our refuge and strength, an ever-present help in trouble.* [2] *Therefore we will not fear, though the earth give way and the mountains fall into the heart of the sea,* [3] *though its waters roar and foam and the mountains quake with their surging.*
> [10] *"Be still, and know that I am God; . . .*

COURAGE UNDER FIRE

¹¹ The Lord Almighty is with us; . . .
(Psalms 46, NIV)

God was hiding me under His feathers—I pictured this based on Psalm 91:4. I could be exhausted, but my God was mighty. It was not my strength, but His. In the same way the eagles can soar over the storm, I was going to soar with my Lord above the storm. *"Be still, and know that I am God."*

but those who hope in the Lord will renew their strength.
They will soar on wings like eagles;
they will run and not grow weary,
they will walk and not be faint.
(Isaiah 40:31, NIV)

Open My Eyes

By the third cycle of chemotherapy the days were becoming very difficult. It was draining all of my energy. Exhaustion and fatigue were the rule, not the exception, those days. I focused on making it through one day at a time or even one step at a time. There were times when even a day or a step seemed too heavy to bear. At those times, I then focused on just one breath at a time.

During chemotherapy I had to keep my body well hydrated to fight exhaustion. My doctor suggested I drink at least 64 ounces of non-caffeinated liquids to help ward off fatigue and to help my body get rid of the drugs once they did their job. I took this very seriously, but there were days that I didn't feel like drinking or eating and ended up in the clinic being intravenously hydrated.

I stopped drinking coffee to ensure I reached the recommended 64 ounces of non-caffeinated liquids every day. Even thought I managed to drink those 64 ounces—and sometimes more—there were moments I felt at night that my eyeballs were firmly stuck to my eyelids. I couldn't open my eyes! It was painful! My mucous membranes didn't have any leftover moisture since the medication was sucking up every bit of it. There were days that I just had to lay and rest. Psalm 23 and Psalm 91 were so close to my heart those times.

Even though I walk through the valley of the shadow of death,
I will fear no evil, for you are with me; . . .
(Psalms 23:4, ESV)

Coping With Exhaustion

He will cover you with his feathers,
and under his wings you will find refuge;
his faithfulness will be your shield and rampart.
(Psalms 91:4, NIV)

One afternoon I was feeling so drained and exhausted that I called Angel and the kids to my bed to kiss them because I was going to fall asleep very early. I was also feeling a little bit uneasy. Alejandro was the last one to leave the room, so I immediately grabbed his arm and asked him to read to me Psalm 91 to help me find rest. He started reading it to me. As I was hearing his tender voice and the words of the Psalm, I started to feel calm. I told him to keep reading until the very end even if I fell asleep. The words of that Psalm in that beautiful voice were the last thing I wanted to treasure and store in my heart at that moment before falling asleep. Then, like a computer, I logged off and went into shutdown mode.

I woke up at one in the morning. I was not feeling good. I felt like I wasn't even breathing . . . but of course I was.

"One breath at a time. One breath at a time . . ." I repeated to myself. "All is good. All is well. My Lord is here."

I tried to open my eyes but couldn't. My eyeballs were stuck to my eyelids and it was painful trying to open them. I always kept a bottle of water on my nightstand so that I could reach it with my eyes closed. Taking one breath at a time, I slowly reached for the bottle. I grabbed it and, after making sure I could hold it, slowly brought it toward me. I took a sip and wetted my fingers to put some water in my eyes. I opened them slowly and in the dark watched the ceiling fan for a while. I turned my head and watched Angel sleeping.

I then asked God to allow me to open my eyes in the morning to see my children again. . . . I made it through the night! God gave me another day and for that I was grateful. I was determined to make the most out of it.

"All is good. All is well," I repeated in my mind again.

I concentrated on taking one breath at a time and on sipping water slowly. I could barely feel my heart beating. I then asked God to allow me to open my eyes in the morning to see my children again.

What happened immediately after that, I don't remember. I guess I fell asleep. I was grateful for one thing when I woke up: I made it through the night! God gave me another day and for that I was grateful. I was determined to make the most out of it.

> *Because you are my help, I sing in the shadow of your wings.*
> *I cling to you; your right hand upholds me.*
> *(Psalms 63:7-8, NIV)*

Strange Episodes

I experienced some strange episodes during this period. I could be sitting in my bed, not being able to sleep. I would walk downstairs and sit on the sofa watching my family and friends like pictures in my mind and suddenly burst into tears. I couldn't explain why. With the leftover energy I had, I cried and cried until I had no more tears or energy left. It was like a sudden earthquake that I couldn't contain.

I could feel guilty for such a moment of weakness, even more when I couldn't explain it. I knew all the time that my Lord was holding me. I cried out for Him to hold me strongly and cover me with His feathers. His presence then was clothing me and after I was drained of my last drop of energy, I remained in awe of His presence. It was not my own strength but His that was going to get me through. I knew that the all-knowing, all-present God of the universe saw me and cared for me in a way that words couldn't explain. Such knowledge was precious to me; too amazing for me to attain.

This is part of the cancer battle. You fight, you get tired, you get hurt, you rest and then regain your energy and balance. Remember, cancer is not the end; it's just something in the way. Adversity is something you may face in your journey, but remember, there is something bigger . . . much bigger. My fellow warrior, you are not alone.

Coping with Uncertainty

Metamorphosis of Uncertainty

Sometimes I felt like an invisible person, walking around without really being there. I felt like a mirror image in the eyes of other people. They were only seeing the outside and not the battle I was fighting every day.

Every day was so uncertain that I learned to find the magic in getting through each day one step at a time. I was starting to feel like a traveler . . . like someone who pays more attention to the journey than the destination. I discovered something attractive about uncertainty. It was the knowledge that God was in control and that I was depending on him every moment.

> *I discovered something attractive about uncertainty. It was the knowledge that God was in control and that I was depending on him every moment.*

I was looking to be the best steward possible of the blessings I had received, giving honor to the One who gave me everything. Want what you already have. Yes, indeed. If I had one more day, I felt blessed.

Instead of focusing on the "what if," I found myself living each moment to the fullest. I was enjoying the eternity behind each step, the wonderful reality of the blessings in my life, the laughter of the simple, the inexplicable strength of a small hug and the certainty of the presence of the ones beside me. The rest was just decoration and vanity.

The Layoff Day

One day my phone rang. It was Angel calling me to tell me that he was called to a meeting at work and he was one of only two people there. By his voice, I knew what he was going to tell me next.

He was told his section was eliminated. He was laid off. I took a deep breath and told him that I loved him.

"When is your last day?" I asked.

"Today. I'm gathering all my things," Angel replied.

His voice was calm. Somehow I thought that he knew that God was preparing us for this.

"God provides," he told me.

"I love you and we are together in this! With all that's happening, I am certain that God will show His grace and glory throughout all this. He just wants to show us," I was resolute.

"I know. I feel the same way," Angel said. "Somehow, I feel calm."

"God provides." "God will provide." That sentiment was the theme throughout the conversation. We had no clue whatsoever what was going to come next. I felt Angel was learning alongside me how to prevail in the midst of uncertainty . . . holding on to the Lord's hand. Our call is primarily to believe and, in the process, to better know the One in whom we believe. God takes care of the rest.

After our conversation, I started praying. The words of Luke 8:50 came to mind:

"Do not be afraid; only believe, . . .
(Luke 8:50, NKJV)

Then other verses began flowing into my heart and mind:

Jesus said to him, "If you can believe, all things are possible
to him who believes."
(Mark 9:23, NKJV)

Immediately the father of the child cried out and said with
tears, "Lord, I believe; help my unbelief!"
(Mark 9:24, NKJV)

The Spirit was telling me to believe. If I had any trace of disbelief I was surrendering it to the Lord. I started trembling because I knew that something was about to occur. I didn't know what it was, but somehow I was certain that God was going to provide. I asked the Lord to prepare our hearts because I felt that we were about to experience a blessing much bigger than our uncertainty. I had no idea what was going to happen, but I was certain more than ever that I could do nothing but keep faith. I only had to lean on God. I said aloud, "Lord, this is for your glory. I'll will listen and believe your Word."

Prayer and faith are correlated. Prayer is not only about expressing one's most inner hopes and wishes; it is also praising and seeking the Lord's will while exercising faith. I then prayed:

"Thank you Lord because in your awesomeness you see me. Oh Lord, help me believe. You are my strength. Help me to discover what you have for me. I'm in your hands. My family is in your hands. You sustain us."

> *Then Jesus said, "Did I not tell you that if you believe,*
> *you will see the glory of God?"*
> *(John 11:40, NIV)*

Amazing words those of John 11:40! I was excited and anxious waiting to see Angel so I could give him a big hug and tell him about my prayer and the verses that had been reaffirmed in my heart.

Journal Entry

Prayer and worship. That is my daily food. My strength. My portion. I also pray with my kids who are 8 and 10 and we take turns in who will lead the prayer. It feels awesome when I hear them elevate their prayers, thanking God for their family and praying for her mom. Prayer and worship is what sustains me every day, every moment.

Peace in the Storm

When Angel was laid off it was as if God had been preparing us beforehand. We had already been praying for God to prepare our minds and our hearts, and to sustain us with His grace. Angel had been feeling uncomfortable at work for weeks and even though we didn't know what was causing this feeling, we sensed that something was going to happen. Because of that, we were already praying and we were at peace because we knew that God had a plan for us.

One day Alejandro said to Angel with obvious sadness and worry in his voice:

Coping With Uncertainty

"Dad, this is so bad. Mom with cancer and now you lose your job."

"Alejandro, don't be afraid. Our trust is in the Lord and He is our provider," Angel said.

Indeed, our trust is in the Lord. God is faithful to his promise. I knew that God was preparing our hearts for the harvest. He doesn't forsake his children.

I was praying constantly for my children, for them to see the powerful hand of God upon us so that they could see that God restores and that God is awesome beyond description. I knew that God had brought us where we were. I trusted that the hand of God would not take you to a place where His grace would not be with you.

> *Now faith is being sure of what we hope for and assurance*
> *about what we do not see.*
> *(Hebrews 11:1, NIV)*

I prayed for my children to feel the Lord's presence and strength in the situation we all were facing. I prayed that their faith would grow stronger so I needed to teach them by my actions and not just with words. I prayed for them to see how the hand of God strengthens us and calms the storm. I wanted them to fix their eyes on the One who loves us and calls us.

> *The Lord is near to all who call on him,*
> *to all who call on him in truth.*
> *(Psalms 145:18, ESV)*

Journal Entry

To the voice of my Lord I listen in the middle of the storm. In the middle of the storm I fix my eyes in Him and reach His hand. He sustains us. He guides us. God is in control: of the cancer, of the peripheral neuropathy, the neutropenia, of our jobs, of our financial situation . . .

The Lord only asks us to have faith "as small as a grain of mustard seed" (Matthew 17:20). I prayed like the man in Mark 9:24, *"Lord, I believe; help my unbelief."*

I prayed for my doctors to have vision and intelligence to make wise decisions. I prayed for each of them so that God could enlighten them.

I prayed, I prayed and I prayed. Below is one of the prayers I wrote in my journal:

> Lord, you are paving the way to show your glory. I'm in awe. Prepare our hearts to receive your blessings and guard us under your feathers.
>
> Take control of this thorn in my life that tries to torment us. Prepare my heart for your great revelation, for your answer. Fit my feet with the readiness that comes from the gospel of peace. Do not allow this thorn to silence me or bend me. My song and praise are for you!
>
> If there is story I have to tell, if there is something to be done, if I have something to say . . . put your words in my mouth. Show me! I stand before you, because you are my Savior, my Redeemer. You are my refuge! You are my strength!
>
> Illness and ailments come to me like raging giants trying to daunt me or intimidate me. As David did, I'll stand firm before these and said: *"You come against me with sword and spear and javelin, but I come against you in the name of the Lord Almighty"* (*1 Samuel 17:45, NIV*). I stand before these and said: "You have no authority here. I am not frightened."
>
> My Lord, my love, strengthen my kids and my husband so that they won't fear. Your presence clothes me and sustains me. In you I believe. In you I trust because you are faithful to your promise, because I have seen your hand in my life. My soul calls to you from the deepest corner of my guts. It calls to you in worship and praise with groans that words cannot express.

Coping With Uncertainty

*In the same way, the Spirit helps us in our weakness.
We do not know what we ought to pray for,
but the Spirit himself intercedes for us
through wordless groans.
(Romans 8:26, NIV)*

I rest in your Word. Cover me within your feathers. Let me touch the edge of your cloak. I'll grab it and I won't let go. Thank you for your embrace.

An Answered Prayer

One morning I was cutting Angel's hair in preparation for a job interview he had later that day. When I was finished he looked so handsome. I did a good job! He was happy and we both prayed together for success in his interview. I was feeling relatively well so I took advantage of that and went to the office. If God gave me the strength to be able to go to work, I was going to use that strength and do my share.

I prayed all morning for the presence of God to be with Angel and for the Lord's guidance in our lives. At some point I looked at the clock and I realized it was already after 11 AM and I thought: "Oh, he's in the job interview right now!" I kept praying. Noon came and went and I still was waiting for his phone call. I was busy at the office, feeling productive and happy and forgot about Angel's phone call. I kept busy for quite a long time before checking my phone yet again. I hadn't realized I had a text message waiting:

"They offered me the job."

I praised the Lord. How great is our God! How amazing is our God! I called Angel immediately. He had two more weeks before he started in his new position I kept thinking, "An answered prayer! An answered prayer right there!"

God is true to his promises and I was glad that He will never stop working in our lives.

COURAGE UNDER FIRE

> **Journal Entry**
>
> Oh Lord . . . if I could just kiss you and hug you big time!

You Choose

When I read Psalm 23, "The Lord *is my shepherd I shall not want,*" all anxiety vanished. Whenever any fear or doubts tried to engulf me, I thought of those words. That Psalm spoke directly to my heart and was refreshment to my soul.

Should you feel any fear, doubt or anxiety in your walk through life read Psalm 23 and meditate on its meaning. You may be overwhelmed sometimes but remember; <u>you</u> can choose <u>your</u> attitude. Choose to listen, choose to believe. You

> *You may be overwhelmed sometimes but remember; you can choose your attitude.*

may not have control of what you are going through: treatment side effects, body changes, medical results, the storm around you . . . but you can choose your attitude.

When in doubt, trust the Lord with all your heart and rest in His promises. Feed your faith from the Word of God. Not just read the Bible, study it and your doubts will fade. Even if you don't see a clear path now, God will give you vision—the ability to see beyond your current circumstances. See yourself as an empty vase to be filled with the Lord's presence and revelation. See yourself as you want to be.

I found myself fighting fear and uncertainty every day. When those feelings knocked on the door, I prayed. I prayed and remembered Psalms 23 and 91. Those Psalms are powerful. As the fear subsided I was ready again to fight the "good fight" with faith and strength.

I prayed constantly and God answered. He gave me the courage to act, to make decisions, to ask questions, the ability to act despite the uncertainty ahead of me. I was fighting an unseen enemy and I saw myself as David facing Goliath (refer to 1 Samuel 17:20-47). Cancer was a giant that was mocking my faith, trying to intimidate me, trying to make me afraid. I stood my ground and declared: "You won't defeat me, you won't vanquish my soul. I will face you in this battle. I will choose to listen and believe the Word of God."

Unfinished Chemotherapy?

After I hadn't reacted well to the treatment with Taxol my doctor recommended a combination of three chemotherapy drugs: Cyclophosphamide, Methotrexate and 5 Fluorouracil. This combination is commonly referred to as CMF, named for the first letter of each of the drugs involved. The new chemo protocol was supposed to last 3 cycles spaced two weeks apart.

As I already just completed 3 weeks of Taxol treatments, we were unsure whether to go for 2 or 3 CMF treatments. Because of the aggressive cancer I had, my doctor recommended me to go with the full 3 CMF cycles, as there was no way to determine if the Taxol cycle had had any benefit as an adjuvant therapy[1]. She was going to monitor me closely to see how my body reacted.

My body did not react well. I was exhausted and not recovering as expected. In addition, my blood levels were going crazy. "Your bone marrow is telling us something," Dr. Kazhdan said. Therefore, she decided to cease the chemo.

The question in my mind was: "Now what? What about me and this incomplete chemotherapy treatment?" By starting and stopping my chemo over and over again I was in uncharted territory in terms of long-term survival statistics. Dr. Kazhdan then told me that we were going to discuss the hormonal therapy later on. For now, radiation therapy was recommended. She was going to send my data to a radiation oncologist to evaluate the situation and determine if I could have any benefit with radiation treatment. Regarding hormonal therapy, the doctor was going to present me alternatives and recommendations so I could make an informed decision. "Too much information, too much to consider . . ." I was overwhelmed.

Upon my insistence, the doctor agreed to discuss the next steps further to satisfy my curiosity. After our discussion she told me to rest for a week, consider all the information she had given me, and come up with more questions. I concurred. There was too much information for my chemo affected brain to digest right then and there.

COURAGE UNDER FIRE

Since I was unable to finish the second regime of chemo (Taxol), nor the 3rd regime (CMF), I felt submerged in a vast sea of uncertainty and uneasiness. I was now off the statistical charts that show the increased benefit of a given adjuvant therapy[1] as reducing the chance of breast cancer recurrence. I only had my faith in God's presence in that entire situation, my Lord's assurance. I felt God was preparing me so that I could rest in His grace and His promises, and not rely on statistics or science. "He is the one that holds my hand," I said. "God is my shepherd, I shall not want."

> *I felt God was preparing me so that I could rest in His grace and His promises, and not rely on statistics or science.*

"My grace is sufficient for you, . . .
(2 Corinthians 12:9, NIV)

In the meantime, I was living every minute of the pathway, the eternity behind every step, the uncertainty of the way, the wonderful reality of the blessings that accompanied me . . . the inexplicable strength found in true hugs . . . the certainty of the presence of the One and the ones who were by my side.

Journal Entry

I'll fight. I'll keep on fighting . . . No time to grieve.

Over those days I listened the Chris Tomlin song "Our God" over and over again. I sang along out loud with all my heart. The song is one of praise and affirmation that God is mighty, great and strong. It is an affirmation of the words:

If God is for us, who can be against us?
(Romans 8:31, NIV)

Coping with Anxiety

Relying on His Grace

I kept a list of songs that "spoke to me" and listened to them constantly. They fed my spirit and my prayers. They were songs that inspired me during my treatment. One of them, "Always," sung by Kristian Stanfill, always reminded me of the Psalms that comforted me and described the Lord as my helper, my strength, my hope and my refuge. I also had the Word of God close to my heart. These Psalms, in particular, gave me comfort:

> *But I will sing of your strength, in the morning I will sing of*
> *your love; for you are my fortress,*
> *my refuge in times of trouble.*
> *(Psalms 59:16, NIV)*

> *Keep me safe, my God, for in you I take refuge.*
> *(Psalms 16:1, NIV)*

When I sang with my soul and meditated on many Bible verses, I felt the presence of the Lord. I breathed and acknowledged:

"He's taking care of me. I'm in His hands, in His hands marked by love."

Both friends and strangers asked me to tell them my story. They told me that my faith during this situation and my blog postings were inspiring them. They wanted to know more. At first, I didn't know what to tell them. It was not easy to go back to my darkest and difficult moments. But then again, those were the moments in which I felt so intensely that Jesus had me in His hands and was carrying me. Those were the moments when I let go of all the things I was holding onto, and emptying myself for the Lord.

I was experiencing what it was to let go of all the things I treasured. We often think that when we talk about learning to let go of things we hold onto so eagerly, we talk about material things. I realized that this goes much further. I slowly started to let go of my sense of security and confidence in my finances, in my work, in my savings and instead, trust and take refuge in the Lord. I then realized how strongly I was trying to hold on to my children and my husband. "Fear" knew this and constantly attacked me that way . . . through the fear of loss. This only added more anxiety to my heart. I needed to understand that in the same way the Lord took care of me, I had to trust that He would take care of them; they were not mine but blessings shared with me by His grace. I had to trust and rely on God's grace and love, and let them go. I had to surrender them to His hands and trust Him. The walk with the Lord begins with one step and continues with the same step—faith.

I was willfully choosing to trust God. There were times when I had to focus on the certainty of His presence and the certainty that He was my light in the darkness; He was going to show me the way. In those moments I became an empty vase and the Lord filled me with a peace beyond all understanding:

> *Be anxious for nothing, but in everything by prayer and*
> *supplication, with thanksgiving, let your requests be made*
> *known to God; and the peace of God, which surpasses all*
> *understanding, will guard your hearts*
> *and minds through Christ Jesus.*
> *(Philippians 4:6-7, NKJV)*

I was there in my weakness, trusting the Lord and putting all in His hands. I was feeling that I was His and that He was there holding me. In the middle of my severe neutropenia, in the middle of my anguishing pain, in the middle of my fatigue, His presence restored me and rejuvenated me from within. He gave me the strength to praise and worship Him in the darkest moments.

Many times I closed my eyes and concentrated on taking one breath at a time, just one breath at a time. There were times that I was so exhausted I felt as if I would fall asleep and wouldn't be able to wake up again. In those moments I prayed and worshiped the Lord without words. I was too tired to form words to echo my thoughts. I would fall asleep with the determination in my heart to not fear, to keep my eyes on the Lord, to listen to His voice. "This is for your glory, Oh Lord," I affirmed.

When I would awake I would feel a little better. I would smile and praise Him again.

> *For our light and momentary troubles are achieving for us*
> *an eternal glory that far outweighs them all.*
> *(2 Corinthians 4:17, NIV)*

Faith and Emotions

I am convinced that when you reach out to God in faith, His presence will be there whether you feel it or not. This understanding was precious to me. It didn't matter how I felt, the certainty that He was there with me fed my spirit and faith. It was not about being happy, but rather about keeping a positive attitude and choosing to believe. Emotions come and go, but His presence is certain—unchanging.

I remember a moment in which I couldn't control my emotions and in a way, they betrayed me. My husband was on travel for his new job and my friend Blanca came from Puerto Rico to give me a hand with the kids and to just to be there with us for a few days. We were so excited about her visit! I was so happy. My kids were too, and were jumping all over the place. Even the dog was happy! By the time her visit came to an end, I was incredibly happy and thankful: "Thanks my friend for the magic moment of your visit." One of the best memories I have from her visit was the moment I saw that yellow cab approaching. I prayed thanking God and my friend for the gift of that memory.

While praying and being thankful for those moments, I suddenly started feeling like exploding in tears. Blanca was going to return to her family in Puerto Rico in just a few hours and in an instant I felt as if missing my love ones altogether. I tried to compose myself but didn't know what to do with the emotions inside of me. I just started crying like a little girl. I started feeling guilty because I was crying when I should be grateful and that made me feel even worse. I kept on sobbing. I couldn't contain myself. I suddenly felt so sad. The more I tried to control my emotions, the worst I felt, so I stopped trying and let it go.

I was many miles away from many relatives and close friends. They were over there, and I was over here battling for my life. My parents were far away. Suddenly I was feeling so weak, so alone. Angel was traveling and not there to comfort me. I didn't want anybody to see me in that state. I then prayed: "Oh God! Take this loneliness and throw it far away from me. Let your presence stand firm all around me."

Even though I felt somehow guilty for crying in front of my Lord, I knew that my Lord is love. Then I heard His whisper . . . "It's all right."

Coping With Anxiety

I had been fighting for so long; I suppose I was simply exhausted. I thought about the fact that my doctor was going to stop the chemotherapy because my body just couldn't take it any more. All that uncertainty was before me. Who would understand? Then, I heard my Lord's voice like a soft thunder: "It's all right . . . Be still and know that I am God."

Do not feel guilty if your strength falls apart for a moment. Let yourself cry sometimes. It may refresh your soul, but don't lose yourself in anxiety. Take heart, take courage, and keep fighting the good fight of faith.

Do not rely on your emotions to guide your faith or to determine whether you feel that God is with you. Whenever you feel troubled, exercise the faith and cling to the Word of God with all your might. The Lord will empower you and the anxiety will melt away. Grasp the cloak of the Lord. Hold on tight. Let His grace carry you.

Journal Entry

My God, forgive my weakness. My eyes are fixed in you. My hand is reaching yours. Thanks for not letting go. You hold me strong. It is like an explosion of light inside and around. Then, I'm strong. You enlighten my way.

Cast all your anxiety on him because he cares for you.
(1 Peter 5:7, NIV)

Oh Lord, your word is precious to me. Let's carry on.

He makes me lie down in green pastures,
he leads me beside quiet waters,
he refreshes my soul. He guides me along the right paths
for his name's sake.
(Psalms 23:2-3, NIV)

COURAGE UNDER FIRE

For no matter how many promises God has made, they are "Yes" in Christ. And so through him the "Amen" is spoken by us to the glory of God.
Now it is God who makes both us and you stand firm in Christ. He anointed us, set his seal of ownership on us, and put his Spirit in our hearts as a deposit, guaranteeing what is to come.
(2 Corinthians 1:20-22, NIV)

[34] Therefore do not worry about tomorrow, . . .
[33] But seek first the kingdom of God and His righteousness, and all these things will be given to you as well.
(Matthew 6:34&33, NIV)

Coping with Appearance

During my breast cancer journey I experienced that <u>real</u> strength comes from the inside, not from your muscles. I realized that self-acceptance and self-esteem were crucial. I had to be proud of "who I am" and "how I look" to be able to wear a smile filled with hope each day. How could I fight and inspire hope if I was not content with myself?

The mastectomy, the cancer treatment and breast reconstruction were not merely medical procedures. It was a whole process; a slow process of constant physical change. During my bilateral mastectomy I had tissue expanders[1] implanted because at that time we were uncertain if I was going to undergo radiation therapy. Radiation is best administered before getting the "permanent" implants because they may be damaged by radiation. I had the tissue expanders for months. They were slowly filled with saline solution during a period of time to retain the elasticity of my skin in preparation for eventual breast implants. Boy, I hated the expanders! They were uncomfortable and the appointments to fill the expanders were like facing the boogie man. Immediately after the "refill" I had to deal with the tightness and pain in my chest and I was already tired of pain. For a few days after each appointment my chest felt too tight. I couldn't even sit straight and had difficulty sleeping. Even hugs would scare me! Many times my poor boys approached to give me hugs and I had to immediately warn them: "Watch out! Watch out! Careful! Careful!" I had difficulty even being in a car with the moves and turns— wearing the seatbelt was particularly painful. There were many days that I had to tell Angel not to look at my face when he was driving to avoid stressing him out.

Many might think that breast reconstruction after a mastectomy is something comparable to "regular" breast implants surgery—at least that was what I thought. I had to wait approximately 11 months after the mastectomy to have the tissue expanders removed and the implants inserted. Even then, the reconstruction was not complete. While the breasts were "growing" with time—as the expanders were gradually filled—I realized they were not growing evenly. My scars and chest were still healing from the bilateral mastectomy and it was not a uniform process. Strange as it may sound, sometime the breasts were not where they supposed to be. However, even with the setbacks and discomfort, I was glad that health insurance companies are now required to include breast reconstructive surgery after a mastectomy as part of breast cancer treatment—as far as I know, this was not an option for the first breast cancer warriors.

I was dealing with the aftermath of the bilateral mastectomy and slow recovery process, with the chemotherapy and its side effects—and soon with radiation—and with the slow breast reconstruction process. The nurse comforted me telling me that soon I would have implants and that these would be more comfortable and would look more natural. For the time being I had to live with the tissue expanders and the odd appearance they gave me. I decided to look at the bright side of this; I didn't have to wear a bra all the time, as they were really tied to my chest cavity and barely moved. I decided to wear loose clothing—sometimes a larger size to feel comfortable. I repeated to myself: "This is temporary. All is well."

My whole body was changing. I looked at my face in the mirror. I looked at my body. How much I had changed in a couple of months! I didn't have hair, I didn't have eyelashes, I didn't have eyebrows, I looked pale, my breast looked all weird with the tissue expanders and the scars, my hands looked old, my nails were dark, my toe nails were dull. But when I looked at my eyes in the mirror, I saw myself. I saw a warrior. I was still me. I smiled and told myself, "Keep kicking cancer's ass! Don't be fooled Yilda! Don't be fooled!" I smiled at myself and suddenly, I was all beautiful.

> I looked at my face in the mirror. I looked at my body. How much I had changed in a couple of months! . . . But when I looked at my eyes . . . I saw myself. I saw a warrior. I was still me. I smiled and told myself, "Keep kicking cancer's ass! Don't be fooled Yilda! Don't be fooled!"

I just had to accept myself as I was. I was starting to gain some weight and that worried me. The doctor told me that could be caused by the medication. I started walking every time I felt able to do so. I started pushing myself to walk a little more each time. As I used to tell my kids: "If it's too hot, take your cap off . . . don't complain. There is always an option." I looked at my options and took action. If I didn't lose some weight it didn't matter because at least walking made me feel good that I was able to exercise and improve my overall health. Walking also gave me time to talk and share many things with my older son, as he decided to walk regularly with me. When we walked, we talked and laughed about different things. The important thing was that we were spending valuable time with each other. The initiative of walking was not only about regaining stamina and taking control of my weight and health. It was about maintaining a positive attitude and sharing good times with one whom I love dearly.

Every morning I faced myself in the mirror. I looked into my own eyes and gave thanks to the Lord for another day. I had to be content with myself. I was then able to feel more strengthened. I was even able to praise the Lord for my condition as it was driving me closer to His glory. "Lord, may your glory shine in me. Yours is the glory and honor."

I was depending on the Lord each day. I couldn't be in greater hands.

"If this means that the glory of the Lord be manifested, so be it. I'm your instrument and You are the master playing a sublime melody."

Since I play the violin, I saw myself as the violin and the Lord as the master violinist who was refurbishing and tuning the instrument with so much love and tenderness, for that violin to make a beautiful sound, a wonderful melody in His hands. I couldn't be more honored!

> I saw myself as the violin and the Lord as the master violinist who was refurbishing and tuning the instrument with so much love and tenderness, for that violin to make a beautiful sound, a wonderful melody in His hands. I couldn't be more honored!

I have to admit that there were times when I was in a meeting or talking to someone and I had the tendency to hide my hands. Because of the chemo my hands were always dry and my nails looked grey and withered. I didn't want people to think that I didn't take good care of my hands or that I had a nasty fungus of some sort. I took good care of my hands, though, to ensure they were clean and moist—or else they would look like dried raisins. I tried in those occasions to keep my chin up and maintain eye contact. Don't feel sorry for yourself or how you look, ensure that people see in yourself a warrior, and they will respect you for who you are and won't care how you look.

Love Transcends

There are two great commandments that Jesus discusses in Matthew 22:37-39. The first one is, *"Love the Lord your God with all your heart, all your soul, and all your mind."* The second one is, *"Love your neighbor as you love yourself."* These verses made me realize I had to accept myself and learn to love the person I was seeing in the mirror. The better I accepted myself, the better I was going to love others.

Acceptance was a process, not a one time event. I let Angel and others take pictures of me. I sometimes even took pictures of myself to learn to accept my new look that changed week after week. Looking at my pictures while going through all these changes helped me to accept myself and see myself as a warrior; an honorable warrior that shouldn't be ashamed of the battle wounds.

I looked at pictures of me after cutting my hair before my chemotherapy as a way to prepare myself for the imminent hair loss. I looked at pictures of myself without hair, without eyelashes, without eyebrows, with wigs on, with hats, with headscarves . . . and I always strived to smile in each of them. I wanted to see myself happy no matter what. And in fact, I <u>was</u> full of happiness and joy. I was there in the pictures with my family, among my friends, among the ones I love and care about. I started counting my blessings that far outweighed the things that were missing. Want what you already have, that way you will be content. That way, you will always be rich.

I played with my looks. I wore headscarves and matched them with hats. I have always been a fan of hats and now I had a very good excuse to wear them often. I never colored my black hair before so I bought myself a reddish-brown wig. Whenever I felt like having fun I wore my reddish-brown wig. I chose to accept and love myself.

The words about loving your neighbor *"as you love yourself"* not only called me to respect and be satisfied with myself, but also to praise and be grateful to the Lord. In fact, I started to love others even more. By loving others, I felt a tremendous urge to spread the Word of God and His faithfulness. I needed to share the blessings of His presence in my life and how He was strengthening me and giving me peace in the midst of my cancer fight. I just couldn't keep God's blessings to myself. I needed to take action and spread the Word. I couldn't be silent.

Whenever I had the chance to give a word of hope and strength to someone, I did it with love. My ability to hug, to care for others, to pray for others even more than for myself, increased. I found myself filling out prayers request cards at my church for other people I knew. I prayed for people that were fighting disease. I prayed for others' health, direction, strength, protection, and even for salvation and restoration. I prayed for my husband to be filled with the strength that only God provides because he was juggling his job duties with my health issues, the kids and household tasks. I prayed for my kids, for them to be sheltered beneath the wings of the Lord and for them to grow in the knowledge of God's Word, love, majesty and righteousness. Praying for others gave me the peace to understand and live each day with the knowledge that God was control.

I realized a powerful synergy in those two great commandments of Jesus. By loving God with all my heart, my soul and my mind, I wanted to seek Him more through His Word and the more I discovered His love, I loved Him more and more. By loving others as myself, I started accepting myself no matter what this cancer treatment was doing to me. I was content and my strength as a warrior increased. I was ready to fight the cancer each day with a positive attitude fed by faith. By loving others, I was not isolating myself in the crisis. I was not hiding my cancer experience. Cancer was not something to be ashamed of or something to grieve, but a tool to put myself in the hands of God Almighty and share His presence with others. By loving others, I also experienced a deeper acceptance of others, no matter their religious creed or particular situation. I felt the freedom to share my love of God without fear or prejudice. I had a huge gift of redemption to share! Jesus is not religion. Jesus is life. I had a gift of life to share. I felt the love of others by listening to them and respecting them. By loving others I planted the seed of love and prayer, letting the power of the Word and the love of God to flourish in others' hearts. By loving others I didn't waste time discussing differences or debating matters of faith. In love, I was listening to them, sharing with them, and laughing with them.

Coping With Appearance

Life is too short to harbor resentment about what others did to me or to my family, or what others don't do or didn't do for me. By loving, I experience a sense of freedom through forgiveness. By loving others I prayed for others, sometimes even more than for myself, and experienced a sense of peace beyond my understanding. A peace to walk each day knowing that God is in control, a strength to face each day and to battle with honor the "good fight" with God's armor. Knowing that God was in control gave me more love toward the One who protects me. So by loving God, I love myself, love others, and love God even more. The love of God transcends.

Stand up. Know what you can do and can offer and forget about what others may think about you. True beauty is not an outward appearance; don't be deceived. True beauty comes from within.

Coping with Radiation

This Is Not over Yet

My chemo treatment was over, but the possibility of radiation therapy loomed over me. I had previously ruled out radiation because I was goig to undergo an aggressive chemotherapy. However, I now had to cope with the fact that my treatment was not yet over and with the likely radiation therapy to come.

I hated the possibility of radiation treatment. I thought I might hate it even more than chemo. Again, I decided to put my trust on God and put my prayers before Him. I firmly held on to His voice: "I'm with you." I didn't know what to feel. Many decisions were still to be made.

It was like being inside the "eye" of a hurricane. The "eye" of a hurricane is that circular area of notoriously calm weather and clear sky at the center of the huge spinning storm. That "eye" is surrounded by a circular "eye wall" that has the storm's strongest winds. I was just getting out of the tremendous turbulence and experiencing some kind of calmness, some kind of relief. I had to choose whether to stay in that quietness and escape, or face the next part of the intense storm.

"Oh Lord, I don't know what to ask you—I prayed—I would pray not to receive radiation . . . but again, I have to pray in your will. Oh Lord, show me how to pray in your will in this circumstance. Wrap me up in your wings. I need you every moment, every step of the way."

The radiation oncologist informed me that based on the aggressive breast cancer I had and given the situation with my chemotherapy treatment, I could certainly benefit from radiation. The potential benefit far outweighed the risks. Previously, the slim benefit that radiation may have provided wasn't worth the pain it would have caused. Now everything had changed. Two different doctors were recommending radiation if I truly wished to decrease the possibility of cancer recurrence. I was faced again with the question, "What do I want to do?"

"What do I want to do?" Of course I didn't want to go through radiation treatment! But I was fighting for my life; I was fighting for more years with my family, to see my kids grow. I couldn't just cross my fingers and hope for the best. I had responsibility for my health; I had responsibility for my family.

Coping With Radiation

"Lord, I ask you for wisdom. Grant me the courage to make this decision. You have been my strength up to here. You will continue to be my strength."

With that conviction I decided to proceed with radiation. At some point during my chemotherapy treatment my plastic surgeon had told me that the two things he hated the most were severe neutropenia and radiation. The first one, severe neutropenia, he hated because of the health complications that it could bring to the recovery process and the potentially serious implications. Because I had experienced severe neutropenia many times, I had already given him all the worries associated with his first most hated thing. I was going to see him soon to let him know that he was also going to have to deal with his second most hated thing, radiation. The final breast reconstruction stage would have to wait.

The Radiation . . . The Trips

I started the radiation treatment with my chin up. The plan was for daily treatment for six full weeks. I had to apply a special lotion to protect my skin several times a day and every week the doctor would check the affected area. At the same time, I was going to begin five years of hormonal therapy.

I scheduled the radiation sessions after work in order to rest after each treatment and be able to go to work the next day. Soon enough, I started to feel the effects. The first one to manifest itself was exhaustion. I was then managing exhaustion on top of the leftover exhaustion from the chemo.

Angel was traveling a lot with his new job, often every other week. Sometimes he was away for two weeks in a row, home for a week and then gone again. I had to manage my work, radiation treatment, taking care of the kids, school work, cooking, housework and all the other odds and ends of running a household while Angel was away. He was appreciated in his new job and I was happy about that. I saw in his eyes that he would prefer to be with me while I underwent radiation therapy, but I didn't want him to sacrifice his work again. I told him that for as long as I could make it, I was going to make it. If I had to stay home unable to work, then I was going to stay. I told that if I had to use all my remaining leave there were people at work that would donate leave to me so that I could continue getting paid and remained covered by my health insurance. I was getting close to that point. I kept on praying.

Three weeks into radiotherapy my energy level was continuing to drop. I was starting to feel "roasted." Between getting up in the mornings, getting the kids ready for school, work, the treatment, getting the kids from school, cooking, helping them with school work, getting the house in order for the next day . . . I began to feel burnt-out.

One day I was feeling so bad that I asked Alejandro to help me revise Gabriel's homework, helping him if he had any questions, and to go over reading and spelling assignments with him. Immediately after that, I collapsed into bed and couldn't get up. Alejandro managed to complete his own homework and help his brother with his. He saved the day that day and many others after. At the young age of 10 he took the responsibility to help mom and care for his young brother. Even Gabriel, who was 8, was helping with some housework and trying to keep his room in order. Instead of them asking if I could please bring them something to drink, I was the one having to ask them, and they would kindly reply: "Okay mom. Do you want juice or water?"

I was grateful to God for them. I always told them that as family we had to care for each other and respect each other; and they were doing just that. Moreover, they were happy "to do just that." When Angel returned home I would tell him all the good things the kids did to help and we celebrated.

The day came when I had to ask Angel if he could put his travels on hold until I could finish the radiation treatment. Angel didn't hesitate. He stayed and helped others in the office to get the work done.

Baring My Soul

Angel didn't travel for the next few weeks, but he then had to make one more trip. I was alone again. My skin was burned and hurt when my clothes even touched it in spite of all the lotion I put on. I was so exhausted. It was as if you were running a very long marathon and you know that you are near the end. Your pace is not as strong as when you started; you are getting weak and you may even be limping. You pant for air consistently because you are exhausted, but you know you cannot quit, that you have to keep on going. Everything is in slow motion and you remain with the thought of, "I'm going to do this."

Coping With Radiation

One morning when the kids were already in school I put on some relaxing and inspiring music and went to my room. While listening to the beautiful harp music, I reached for a pen because I wanted to write. I was so very tired, but I prayed and after a while I found the strength to firmly hold the pen and write.

I knew what my heart was about to write. I knew that my Lord also knew what was in my heart. My thoughts were like a march of prayers, hope and a confession. I was baring my soul to God. I started writing:

> Radiation. Half of my chest is burned out. I'm feeling too fatigued. I haven't called work yet. I'm still trying to find the energy to call.
>
> I'm trying to think and not to think. My prayer today is, "Oh Lord, fill me with strength. Let me rest a while in your arms, while you fill me with your strength." Philippians 4:13 is in my mind, "I can do everything through him who gives me strength."
>
> Once more, I find myself thinking about my kids, my children . . . Angel is traveling again. I'm all by myself these days. I cannot hide from you these questions that keep coming into my mind.
>
> I trust fully on their dad to care for them if I'm missing. But who will take care of them if both of us are missing? Who will love them like we do? Who will provide for his spiritual education that focuses in a close relationship with you? Who will cultivate in them the love for the music and encourage them to keep playing violin or the piano or any other musical instrument? Who will keep encouraging them to dream and stand for themselves? Who will love them that much to deny oneself and put them first? Who will raise them with a mission, within a divine mission in the loving fear of you, Oh Lord?
>
> My Lord, take care of them always, whether I'm there or not. May your Spirit guide them and cover them. Embrace them with your presence. May you be all for them.

COURAGE UNDER FIRE

The music stopped. I continued my conversation with God:

> I'm feeling your peace, and my strength is before you. I raise my soul in gratitude to you. I can hear your voice in my soul, "I'm with you."

I could hear my breathing. It was calm and deep. My bare soul continued:

> Forgive my weakness. My eyes are fixed in you; my hand is reaching yours. Thanks for not letting go. I feel your presence holding me firm. It's like an explosion of light inside and around. Then I'm strong. You enlighten my way and then your Word comforts me and your promises lift up my spirit.

Forgive my weakness. My eyes are fixed in you; my hand is reaching yours. Thanks for not letting go.

> *He makes me lie down in green pastures,*
> *he leads me beside quiet waters,*
> *he refreshes my soul. He guides me along the right paths*
> *for his name's sake.*
> *(Psalms 23:2-3, NIV)*

> *For all the promises of God in Him are Yes,*
> *and in Him Amen, to the glory of God through us.*
> *Now He who establishes us with you in Christ and has*
> *anointed us is God, who also has sealed us and given us the*
> *Spirit in our hearts as a guarantee.*
> *(2 Corinthians 1:20-22, NKJV)*

One More Day to Be Thankful

Many times I asked myself what my that last day of treatment was going to be like. After 10 long months of intensive treatment—surgeries, chemotherapy and radiotherapy—I was counting down my last days of radiation; I was taking each day slowly and patiently. When the last day of radiation finally arrived, the medical staff threw me a surprise party full of joy and hugs. I was both exhausted and happy. I was grateful because the Lord sustained me all the way. He strengthened me and allowed me to be surrounded with friends and loved ones who were with me during my journey. They were there through prayers, encouraging words, amazing acts of love and continuous support. I thanked God for all and every one of them.

I was still recovering from the effects of chemotherapy and radiation and, although I felt tired, I also somehow felt strong. On my way home, I thanked God for His presence, for His Word of wisdom. In my weakness He was my strength and He gave me courage. Whenever the darkness blurred my path, He was my light, my compass. He dissipated the fear with his peace that surpasses all understanding. He held me. He never let go.

Psalm 23 took on a new meaning for me and I started reading it to my kids constantly. I thought, "life is so fragile, that I have to share with them the most precious thing I have, which is the Lord's presence in our lives." During this time my older son had minor surgery to remove a lipoma—a benign tumor—from his neck. Before he was taken into surgery, I asked him if he wanted to pray. Not only did he want to pray, but he also told me he wanted me to whisper Psalm 23 in his ear. We put our foreheads together and whispered the Psalm 23 to each other, then shared a smile. It was not just another moment; it was a precious moment. It was awesome that he wanted to hear that Psalm before facing the unknown.

Returning to my initial thought, "What did my last day of treatment feel like?" I felt excited, although exhausted. I felt thankful. All I wanted to do was to rest for a while . . . and after that, rest a little bit more. Later, I would celebrate. As a matter of fact I was already celebrating an overwhelming sense of relief. I had done it!

> ### *Journal Entry*
>
> I know God's work in me has not finished. I would have never imagined I would be transformed by his grace. I hear the laughter of my kids in the distance, and I breathe in joy. Lord, we are all in your hands.

Coping with the "Leftovers"

Chemotherapy and radiation had taken a tremendous toll on my body and it took some time before I was back to "my old self." My body needed to heal slowly from the "leftovers" of the treatment. My blood results were still not normal, but that was okay considering all I had undergone. Exhaustion, although not constant, was going to be my companion for approximately a year after I finished treatment. Additionally, the hormonal therapy I was receiving also had that "complementary" tiredness along with the "main entry."

At work, everybody was happy because I could finally return to my regular duties. At least that was what I expected from myself. However, it was difficult to fully engage again. The medical appointments were still ongoing, if less frequently, and I still had "things" to watch out for. For some time I was still very sensitive to bright light and more susceptible to allergies and my eyes would constantly become watery. I was still managing peripheral neuropathy along the way and dealing with the fact that when I had to be out in the sun, I knew that my body would soon start "complaining."

Peripheral Neuropathy

I had to cope with peripheral neuropathy, which I developed during chemotherapy, for approximately two years after stopping the chemo. At the beginning of the second chemotherapy regime peripheral neuropathy was bothersome, but not overly so. In a matter of approximately three weeks, however, it suddenly became much worse. It was as if I was being attacked by millions of fire ants. Sometimes I would feel electrical shocks in my hands, arms, neck, back and feet. If I walked for more than ten minutes, I would almost go crazy; I had to sit on the floor no matter where I was. Holding the steering wheel was painful because of the burning-like sensation. Even putting my hands into my pockets was unpleasant as any direct contact of my hands with fabric was painful. In fact, I could barely dress myself.

One day the peripheral neuropathy became unbearable, incapacitating. I was doing some cleaning around the house, sweeping and vacuuming, when suddenly my hands and feet turned red and started to feel like they were burning. I stopped what I was doing. It didn't go away like it always had before so. I started to get frantic. I told my husband I was going to fill the bathtub with cold water to soak my arms and feet. The moment my feet touched the water they burned even more. The feeling was so unbearable that I couldn't even walk on the carpet. I started crawling with my knees and elbows to get into bed and called Angel nearly in tears. I told him to call the doctor immediately. I thought I might be having an allergic reaction. I couldn't move. I was stiffly laid in bed face down with my arms and legs extended muttering and singing songs in my mind to try to calm myself down.

When the peripheral neuropathy got to that point the doctor immediately suspended the chemo regime and referred me to a neurologist. We were hoping that there was no permanent damage to my peripheral nerves. Luckily, after some test, it was determined that the damage was temporary, but it was hard to say how long it would take to heal. The neurologist told me that sometimes depending on the extent of the damage, the nerves could take up to two years to recover. I was given a medication to manage the pain by decreasing the number of nerve signals to calm down my overly sensitive nerve cells. With the new medication I was able to endure the pain. However, the pain medication had its own bothersome side effects to deal with. For a long time, I could still feel the neuropathy, especially when driving, when exercising, walking or when exposed to sun, but I preferred to tolerate it and manage it rather than increase my medication.

Chemo Brain

Wait a minute! What? You got it right: "Chemo brain."[1]

During and after the chemo treatment I noticed that I was becoming forgetful; it was difficult to concentrate and that it was hard to perform mental calculations. I was getting worried and one day I mentioned this to one of my nurses jokingly telling her that I might be already getting older or I had "chemo brain." She looked at me and said that she didn't think it was age because I was still so young. I thanked her for that remark! She then told me that she had heard the term "chemo brain" before to refer to that lack of focus.

I was not only experiencing lack of focus and mental sharpness, but also experiencing "word loss." I would be talking and suddenly go "blank." A full year after the treatment this was still happening. It was especially noticeable when I was helping my kids with their homework. They were able to do mental math easily while I would just draw a blank. For a while I resolved not to do mental math to avoid feeling like I had lost something, but I didn't want to give up entirely. I found some apps for my phone to help me practice memory and cognitive skills regularly.

Before, it had not been difficult to memorize new songs to play on my violin or my piano. Now it was becoming very difficult. I didn't want this to frustrate me. I told myself that I didn't care and that I was going to keep on trying like I did before, step by step.

My "chemo brain" played tricks on me again and again. Sometimes, when getting blood drawn, I didn't even know which was my left arm or right arm. This was important because I couldn't use my left arm for either blood pressure taking nor blood work. On my first surgery I had some lymph nodes removed on the left side and I couldn't use that arm in order to avoid lymphedema[2]. My solution was to wear a commemorative breast cancer awareness pink bracelet on my left wrist.

I did some research on my own about "chemo brain." I discovered that many cancer patients have experience this lack of concentration or forgetfulness after cancer treatment. Unfortunately, there are still some doctors that trivialize this and make their patients feel that it is all in their heads. I resolved not to talk about this with anyone. I was determined to face my limitations and to focus on my abilities.

> *I was determined to face my limitations and to focus on my abilities.*

"Chemo brain" was not an excuse to apologize, to blame it for things I was experiencing; what others might call limitations. It was just another reality with which I had to cope with a positive attitude. To me, I wouldn't mind to be mocked about losing my mental math and speech ability if I get to see my kids grow up and get to share with others the blessings that were given to me.

Journal Entry

Think about your abilities . . . not your limitations.

Early Menopause And "Funny-Looking" Nails

Because the cancer cells were "feeding" off the natural estrogen in my body, I was a good candidate to benefit from hormonal therapy. This therapy was intended to further reduce the chance for breast cancer recurrence. The hormonal "cocktail" I was receiving to suppress the production of estrogen brought with it early menopause. Not only was I experiencing hot flashes and night sweats, but also possible early osteoporosis and joint discomfort. To protect me from osteoporosis I had to take an IV medication every six months for a while. The best preventive measure was to keep active.

My nails turned dull at the beginning of the chemotherapy and then grayish. I had to be very careful with my hands to protect the nails from falling off so I kept them very short throughout my whole treatment. On my toes, the nails were even worse. The doctor told me that, as with my hair, the nails would recover eventually and new nails would grow back. In my case, my nails took a few months to fully recover.

My Poor Liver

Laboratory appointments were a must for medical follow-ups. In the first after-chemo imaging, there were some "protein deposits" evident on my liver. The doctor told me that that was a result of the chemotherapy. With time, my liver would return to normal. In the meantime, I had to try to limit the intake of acetaminophen and use ibuprophen instead when necessary.

"The liver?" I thought. I never thought about my liver before and its function. I remembered my biology courses with respect to the liver location, but that was all I remembered, so I did a search and found out that the liver serves many vital functions in the body. One of the most important is to filter toxic substances from the blood, including alcohol and many different medications such as chemotherapy drugs, antibiotics and acetaminophen. I found out that the liver works somewhat like Superman: detoxifying chemicals and metabolizing drugs; making proteins important for blood clotting; storing vitamins, minerals, proteins, fats and sugar from your diet; helping in the absorption and digestion of fats and providing a way for the liver to eliminate waste products. No wonder my poor liver suffered! Superman had been very busy!

After learning about the liver and its many important functions I became a little concerned. I started treating my liver as if it was my best buddy. I started focusing on good nutrition. I started seeing the food like a scanner—good things versus bad things; things that matter versus things that do not benefit my body. I was really happy when my liver panel test results finally returned as "normal."

My Long-Gone Lost-Friend

My hair started to come back very soft and very thin. Baby hair is what I called it. Because I had removed from sight all the things that would remind me of my hair as soon as I lost it, now I was looking everywhere for hairbrushes. Among the things women always have is a favorite hairbrush. When I had enough "fur" to start brushing, I grabbed that hairbrush and said:

"Hello hairbrush! It's been a while . . .! Have you missed me? Now back to work, my friend. Do something for my baby hair! Yeah!"

"Mom. Are you talking to your hairbrush?" I heard one of my boys comment from the other room, and then I heard some giggles.

THE AFTERMATH

Dealing with the Aftermath

By the time I approached the end of my aggressive cancer treatment, I felt a mix of emotions. I was feeling relief and worry. I experienced a pressure from on other's expectations—or from my own—to return to my normal self as I was before the cancer, to see the words "The End" on a big screen and hear victory music. But after going through that battle fighting for my life, knowing that there were milestones still to reach and knowing that some fellow cancer warriors were deeply wounded or lost in their own battles, it was not easy for me to face the transition to my "new normal." I felt as a soldier returning from war. I found that I was lacking the energy and the drive to immediately fit back into my "normal" life.

This chapter goes beyond the aftermath of cancer diagnosis and treatment. This is not only about the aftermath of cancer, but also about the aftermath of any misfortune or situation that could impact your life dramatically for a new turn.

Facing adversity with determination and resilience is a personal challenge. It is a choice to be made constantly...

Facing adversity with determination and resilience is a personal challenge. It is a choice to be made constantly, an attitude that looks forward.

Practice Resilience

Resilience is a process. It is related to how you deal with difficult events and drastic changes in your life. It is an ongoing process that requires determination, a positive attitude, time and effort. Resilience is sometimes described as "the ability to bounce back" from difficult experiences, adversity or trauma.

Resilience is what allowed me to deal with the "weirdness" that I experienced during and after my cancer treatment, after the reconstruction process and while undergoing hormonal therapy. The "weirdness" was not physical but also emotional.

I found myself with unanswered questions, dragging on the leftovers of the treatment and facing an early menopause and the whole ten yards associated with it. I was taking a medication to help me cope with the peripheral neuropathy that I developed as result of the chemo treatment. Although I knew it was temporary, my body had not yet recovered even after a year. Occasionally it was hard for me to concentrate in my daily routine and I experienced dizziness. That neuropathy medication, however, had another benefit in helping me manage the inopportune and uncomfortable "hot flashes" and "night sweats" of menopause, although it did not eliminate them. Many times I couldn't sleep because of the "night sweats." In other occasions the "hot flashes" showed up during professional meetings and the very noticeable redness of my face and ears raised attention. In those embarrassing occasions I was concerned I would send the wrong message with my reaction to what was being said. On top of that, I sometimes felt an inexplicable exhaustion. I was also dealing with a slight weight gain from the medication in spite of all the efforts that I was doing to regain control of my weight. There were too many things, incomplete feelings and challenges to keep facing.

My advice to you in the face of adversity is that you accept both the physical and emotional changes that come with it. In my case, I accepted my "new normal." I want to share the factors and things that helped me and still are keeping me afloat. The main one is that God is not just "up there." He can take an active part in your life and give you the revelation to find purpose in your life and the eagerness to get on with each new day. You only have to let Him in. God wants us to be participants of His grace one day at a time.

> ### *Journal Entry*
> Practice resilience today. Regain your equilibrium and keep moving forward.

Accept Your "New You"

When my hair started to grow back it started coming in in a funny way. I couldn't determine whether it was coming back straight or curled. It was changing with every few millimeters of new growth. One day I had to admit that for having only 1 centimeter (about ½ an inch) of hair, I could still have "bad hair" days. It wanted to do its own thing without paying attention to what I thought it was supposed to look like. But for better or worse, I took it

COURAGE UNDER FIRE

lightly knowing that for the previous 8 months I didn't have to "fight" with my hair.

Accepting your "new you" is more than managing your misfortunes with a sense of humor. It has to do with cultivating a positive self-image. This view of yourself is not about how you look, but about how you want to project yourself. You cannot change what has happened to you, but you can focus on your strengths and abilities. Focus on these and regain your confidence. See yourself through the eyes of God.

> *You cannot change what has happened to you, but you can focus on your strengths and abilities . . . See yourself through the eyes of God.*

This understanding will give you confidence and help you overcome the constant difficulties of the road ahead. As a working mom, it was hard to picture myself trying to cope with the effects of the cancer treatment and its aftermath, my family life—both as mom and wife—and my professional life. It was very easy to picture myself bald, weak, in trouble, in misfortune, but difficult to picture myself carrying that baggage and still taking care of business with determination, hope and joy. I had to be easy on myself and take one step at a time focusing on my strengths, my abilities and what I wanted to accomplish.

Don't forget to get plenty of rest if you need to. My body had gone through a tough process and it was still going through constant changes. I had to remind myself to rest: "Take your time and rest." Be gentle with yourself and take your time to rest and relax. When you are facing all those changes, picture yourself as being on a journey to health and recovery.

Never think you are done with prayer. Feed your faith and keep seeking the One who's standing by your side. Smile constantly to yourself, even if you are tired. Be kind to yourself, reward and compliment yourself for fighting the good battle of faith. You are not alone; there is a mighty warrior with you.

But the Lord is with me like a mighty warrior; . . .
(Jeremiah 20:11, NIV)

Dealing With the Aftermath

Value Encouraging and Positive Interpersonal Relationships

Identify those within or outside your family that care about you and support you. Keep them close to your heart even though they may not be close physically. Nowadays it is very common to connect and relate to others beyond our physical proximity. I cannot share enough how much support I received through social networks. At first, immediately after my cancer diagnosis, it crossed my mind to "disappear" from the Internet and put all my accounts "on rest" for a while. I'm glad God changed that thought. I received such amazing support from people that wanted to pray for me, cheer me up and send me positive thoughts and good energy . . . The list could just keep on going. Sometimes, although I didn't have a direct relationship to someone, I knew through my connections that there were people from many places and other countries praying for me.

Cultivate and foster healthy relationships with the ones close to you. My family, in particular my husband, was—and still is—a tremendous influence to empower my resilience. When I was not feeling myself, or feeling uncomfortable not knowing why, I trained my mind to let him know right away and that I was going to seek distance to avoid hurting the ones I love. With a few deep breaths, I defused the situation and returned to a stable state of mind. His patience, his tolerance and his strong faith in God gave me strength. My family in Puerto Rico and elsewhere was as supportive as if they were right next to me. They were there supporting me and encouraging me through phone calls, messages, cards, and positive notes.

It is very easy when you are going through a process like cancer and cancer treatment—or whatever very difficult situation you may be going through—to lose your composure and hurt the ones close to you that are trying to do the best they know how to care for you. Remember that they do not have a recipe to deal with the situation either. If this happens, take your time to cool off, regain your equilibrium and make an apology if you value that relationship. Don't let the other person assume that you are sorry for what you did or said by acting sorry. In the same way that our actions can be worth more than a thousand words, the words "I'm sorry . . ." carry enormous weight and value, and can start a process of self-healing and overall healing in any relationship. If you feel you need to apologize for something, be specific. If you feel that your reaction was triggered by something the other person said, didn't say, did or didn't do; talk about it. Identify together the triggers that unleash assumptions and an unwanted chain of events in response. Don't be surprised if you receive an apology in return whether needed or not.

> *In the same way that our actions can be worth more than a thousand words, the words "I'm sorry . . ." carry enormous weight and value, and can start a process of self-healing and overall healing in any relationship.*

There were times I saw my husband trying to take care of so many things that I even thought he was trying to fix me—as weird as it sounds—and I just didn't want to be fixed. I only wanted to be heard and for him to acknowledge my feelings without trying to fix them or feeling responsible for making me feel better. We learned to separate situations from the people involved. The situation is the situation and the people involved in it are not the situation; they are just there with you on your side. Cultivate supportive relationships with the ones close to you and that matter to you. Do not hide within yourself; communicate, and reach out.

Supportive connections can extend to how you communicate with your health care team. Create and maintain a healthy relationship with them through communication. Do not expect your doctors and nurses to know all that you are going through; talk, ask, share. Communicate what you are feeling and what you are going through. Over the course of my treatment I discovered that doctors may ask all sort of questions—about work, about the family or the usual, "How have you been?" They do so not only to be friendly, but to find out if there is anything they could help you with. For instance, when I started reducing the dose of one of my medications, I had a lot of difficulty sleeping. It was getting bothersome and frustrating because I found myself getting easily tired at work. This happened night after night and I was getting restless and upset. I was reluctant to mention this to my doctor because I didn't want any more medication—not even to sleep. I was being led by my own assumption and this didn't solve the situation. During one of my regular follow-up appointments I finally decided to share this with my doctor and she recommended I switch the time I was taking the medication from the morning to right before going to sleep. That worked! Share your thoughts and ask questions. Free yourself from assumptions.

Dealing With the Aftermath

I have always said that friends become the extended family that we choose to have around us. Many long-time friends were very close to me during my journey and their encouragement and support meant a lot. I even connected with new people and made new friends in a way I never thought possible. Seeking or accepting help and support from those who care about you will minimize stress, not only during the storm, but also in the aftermath.

Find something that you can share with others. It could be a talent you have, a blessing, a gift, your experience or knowledge. Find a way to share it. There are many civic groups and organizations that can benefit from what you can offer. In serving others not only someone will benefit from your offering, but also you will find joy and meaning in what you do.

We all make mistakes, but avoid the mistake of thinking that you are all alone. First, understand there is a loving God who wants to take an active part in your life and surround you with His presence. As I've pointed out throughout this book it is possible to have an intimate relationship with your creator. Second, identify and cultivate supportive and healthy interpersonal relationships. Lastly, look for support groups and opportunities to serve in your community. Do not hide within yourself. Communicate, take control of your emotions, don't let them control you, and reach out.

Realign Your Goals and Expectations

Once cancer treatment, or whatever rough road you are on is "over," others will have expectations of you. You cannot control that, but you can control the expectations that you have of yourself. Make sure you distinguish between the two. I was faced with my "new normal" and the need to make realistic plans and determinations.

Before the cancer diagnosis, I practiced and played soccer regularly. I also took martial arts with my kids. I was in better shape than I was when I was going through college—at least so I thought. I was feeling strong. Suddenly, I was faced with breast cancer diagnosis, surgeries, chemotherapy and radiation and it all hit me hard. Between the chemotherapy and radiation I tried to get back into exercise routine. I started walking regularly in the nice fall weather. Soon after, I asked my surgeon if I could go back to my previous routine of push-ups. He was emphatic in his reply: "Start slowly and be nice to yourself. We messed a lot with your muscles in there—he pointed to my chest. It takes time to heal. Don't be discouraged or frustrated if you cannot complete one. Just take it easy."

I can tell you that I became frightened when I tried to do just one push-up. The pain was excruciating. It was as if I was lifting the whole world with my arms. I couldn't even complete one! I started repeating to myself: "Not even one! Not even one!" The frustration of what I was able to do once and not able to do now threatened to discourage me. Then I remembered my doctor's words: "Start slowly and be nice to yourself. It takes time to heal. Don't get frustrated."

Healing is a process and involves not only physical healing but also one's state of mind. I had to realign my expectations and set new goals. I was determined to start slowly and to discover "what I can do now" and by doing it and accomplishing it, be ready for more. If I couldn't do an exercise, I stretched, and that felt wonderful. If I couldn't run, I walked and enjoyed the breeze on my face. Little by little you will be doing more; you will be achieving more. Do not give up.

> *The frustration of what I was able to do once and not able to do now threatened to discourage me . . . I had to realign my expectations and set new goals. I was determined to start slowly and to discover "what I can do now" and by doing it and accomplishing it, be ready for more.*

I had heard that you can experience fatigue, trouble sleeping or lack of motivation for more than a year after cancer treatment. Definitely it was like that. I picked up a brochure while I was going through chemotherapy about a non-profit organization called "ThriveWell Cancer Foundation" and their DIVA (Deriving Inspiration and Vitality through Activity) program. The central mission of "ThriveWell Cancer Foundation" is the development of community-based programs that directly enhance the quality of life for cancer patients and survivors. DIVA provides exercise, nutrition and artful healing programs for breast cancer patients and survivors. These programs were created to offer life-saving opportunities to increase the rate of cancer prevention and survivorship. I saw DIVA as an opportunity to regain my balance and strength. I decided to make the call to enroll in the program and start with little steps. With time, I noticed that I was becoming stronger. When doing exercises with a ball, I remembered my "good old days" of playing soccer and continued with the exercise with a smile on my face. At the same time, I found motivation and I met other women pursuing wellness after cancer.

Take your time to adjust your plans to make realistic goals and take the steps to carry them out. Be nice to yourself. Avoid thinking about how you did before and focus on what you can do <u>now</u>. Challenge yourself to discover those things that you can do and enjoy.

Realign Your Priorities

During the transition from being in a raging storm to the aftermath of the storm, I was faced with the need to establish and act upon priorities. I focused more on being intentional in my daily behavior and avoided being drifted by the flow. I was more determined to seek everyday the eternal perspective in every move; the eternal perspective that I can only reach when looking up to God.

My kids were another incentive to help me choose what was important and what was not. When I looked at them, I saw significance, I saw a mission. My new attitude was to be more focused on my purpose than on trivial matters. Now, it is up to me to determine what it's trivial and what is not. And with that, I feel powerful.

Prioritize fresh air and fun. Cultivate joy in your life and share it with those close to you. Note that I'm not saying to just enjoy life. Enjoyment is more related to the surrounding circumstances. What I mean is to cultivate joy, which is not based on the circumstances but rather is a state of the heart. Seek activities that give you satisfaction and the thought that you are doing something meaningful. Avoid getting caught in the "rat race" and take control of what really matters.

Value those small and simple things that make you smile. When the weather was nice and I was in the car, whether driving or as a passenger, I opened the window and took pleasure of the feeling of my growing hair getting crazy with the wind. My kids and husband laughed at and the crazy dance my hair was doing in the wind. In other occasions I could be talking to my husband over the phone and suddenly—out of the blue—comment, "Did you see the sky? Look at the sky! It looks awesome!"—and immediately started describing it to him.

Make good nutrition one of your priorities and do not compromise. Spend time learning about nutrition. There are many free resources you can use to help you make wise decisions. If you are eating out do not allow the available selection drive what you eat. Value and respect yourself. As crazy as it sounds I even started smiling at my fruit before eating it!

Keep things in perspective. Your long-term goals will determine your steps in the short term. In the same way your steps, your thoughts and your actions can impact or affect your goals. Value your time and how you spend it.

Trust in the Lord with all your heart
and lean not on your own understanding;
in all your ways submit to him,
and he will make your paths straight.
Do not be wise in your own eyes; fear the Lord and shun evil.
(Proverbs 3:5-7, NIV)

But seek first his kingdom and his righteousness,
and all these things will be given to you as well.
(Mathew 6:33, NIV)

Be very careful, then, how you live—not as unwise but as
wise, making the most of every opportunity, . . . Therefore do
not be foolish, but understand what the Lord's will is.
(Ephesians 5:15-17, NIV)

Cultivate Faith

There are mixed emotions in the transition from being a cancer patient to a cancer survivor. I realized that in the beginning I had constant thoughts and fears of recurrence. I had to always be ready for battle, for the battle of faith. When such feelings tried to break-in, I took a firm grasp of my sword and shield.

Dealing With the Aftermath

> *take up the shield of faith, with which you can extinguish all the flaming arrows of the evil one. ¹⁷ Take . . . the sword of the Spirit, which is the word of God.*
> *(Ephesians 6:16-17, NIV)*

I had to fix my eyes on the author of my faith. Keep your eyes on God. As soon as we start focusing on the many things going on "out there," we start losing perspective of where we are, where we stand, what we want for our lives, and what God's will is for our lives. Seek Him with all your heart, mind and soul.

> *Love the Lord your God with all your heart and with all your soul and with all your mind and with all your strength.*
> *(Mark 12:30, NIV)*

Prayer goes along with faith. By prayer I mean asking, communicating and listening. Don't only seek the Lord during hardships, but develop the habit of communicating with Him . . . of listening to Him.

> *"Speak, Lord, for your servant is listening." . . .*
> *(1 Samuel 3:9, NIV)*

Many see the words faith and prayer and associate them with religion or spirituality. This is not about religion or spirituality in a general sense . . . I'm talking about growing into a personal relationship with God. This personal relationship with Christ had transformed my relationship with my family, husband, kids, friends and others. I can say that His work in my life doesn't end here; it grows each and every day.

> *Therefore we do not lose heart. Though outwardly we are wasting away, yet inwardly we are being renewed day by day.*
> *(2 Corinthians 4:16, NIV)*

> *For I am the LORD, your God, who takes hold of your right hand and says to you,*
> *Do not fear; I will help you.*
> *(Isaiah 41:13, NIV)*

It is up to you. How far you want to go and how far you want to grow. Do not let that your worries, the unanswered questions or the abundant and free offer of distractions draw you away from the One who wants to illuminate your way and fulfill your everything.

> *Now faith is the assurance of things hoped for, the conviction*
> *of things not seen.*
> *(Hebrews 11:1, ESV)*

Remember that the word "impossible" is not just a word. It can be an excuse for someone to not try to believe. It can be a self-imposed barrier to prevent your growth beyond what your eyes can see or beyond the blame that you can impose on others for the lack of faith.

It is not simply about "daring to believe," or "believing in yourself" or any other cliché that may sound inspiring. Those only take you to a certain distance. I will tell you this: "Challenge yourself to know God more. Consider Jesus, every one of his words, his actions and reactions. What he said and why he said it. What he did and why he did it. If there is something you don't understand don't give up, keep looking. Ask, seek and knock on the door. You shall find.

> *⁹ "So I say to you: Ask and it will be given to you;*
> *seek and you will find;*
> *knock and the door will be opened to you.*
> *¹⁰ For everyone who asks receives;*
> *the one who seeks finds; and to the one who knocks,*
> *the door will be opened.*
> *¹¹ "Which of you fathers, if your son asks for a fish, will give*
> *him a snake instead? ¹² Or if he asks for an egg, will give him*
> *a scorpion? ¹³ If you then, though you are evil, know how to*
> *give good gifts to your children,*
> *how much more will your Father in heaven*
> *give the Holy Spirit to those who ask him!"*
> *(Luke 11:9-13, NIV)*

It is up to you. How far you want to go and how far you want to grow. Do not let that your worries, the unanswered questions or the abundant and free offer of distractions draw you away from the One who wants to illuminate your way . . .

Dealing With the Aftermath

*Did I not tell you that if you believe,
you will see the glory of God?
(John 11:40, NIV)*

We can easily agree that life is short and that we are not here forever. In Christ we are given an eternal perspective and close relationship with our God since the moment we are born again. We are given a new meaning; we have purpose in the eyes of our Lord. My beloved, look at the bigger picture . . . God in you and you in Him. Let's make every step we take count!

A New Song

I began this journey with Psalms 121 and 42 in my heart and in my mind. Along the way, the Lord's presence was comforting. Now I look at the Psalm 40[1] and I can say I have a new song to offer.

Psalm 40 provides a testimony of God's presence and the blessings experienced throughout difficult situations and how these lead to great joy and a song of praise. In the midst of a struggle one can rely of God's mercy and love to bring restoration and hope.

In the Psalm, the words "patiently wait" do not mean to passively wait. It is not about sitting in a rocking chair to wait for something to happen. The "patient" wait that Psalm 40 refers to is an <u>active</u> wait. It means to put first our hope and will in the Lord and then to walk. It means to put our trust in the Lord and keep doing. It means active prayer and active trust! It is to translate faith into action! It is to seek the presence of the Lord and walk with the certainty of it.

The author of Psalm 40 is comparing his difficult situation with that of being in a *"slimy pit"* and being stuck *"in the mud and mire."* The New King James version uses the words *"horrible pit"* and the New Living Translation uses the phrase "pit of despair." The situation he was experiencing made him feel that he was trapped, stuck, or buried alive, but he chose to put his hope in the Lord and cries out to Him. Then, something amazing happens. I love what comes next: *"he turned to me and heard my cry."* God turns to him, hears him, rescues him and a new song is born in the heart of the one who wrote this Psalm as a living testimony that still remain.

Our God is capable of turning grieve into joy while He embraces us. When we experience His love, His faithfulness and His mercy, a new song of praise is born in our hearts. We become witness of God's grace. The following verses in Psalm 30 cannot illustrate better what I'm trying to say:

> *You turned my wailing into dancing; you removed my*
> *sackcloth and clothed me with joy, that my heart may sing*
> *your praises and not be silent.*
> *LORD my God, I will praise you forever.*
> *(Psalms 30:11-12, NIV)*

A New Song

From these verses I particularly like the phrase, *"my heart may sing and not be silent."* That is one of many things that happen when the Lord walks with us and works His grace on us; we cannot be silent. We are transformed.

In every situation we have to learn to be grateful. We can learn to put music to every tear and live with hope in the middle of conflict. The "new song" doesn't have to wait until everything is calm and the storm passed. We don't have to wait to be grateful.

There is a new beginning! A new road ahead! Hold on to God and sing a new song!

THE TESTIMONY

Hope and Joy in the Dark

When I meditate on what it's like to go through cancer I focus on the hope and joy that God's promises and blessings bring into my life. I also think about the fact that even after cancer treatment no doctor will say, "you are now cured." Instead, you will hear about survival rates. Do not despair; keep God's promises and blessings in mind and have hope.

The hope I'm referring to is not a hope based on desires, but the hope fed by God's Word, in the certainty of God, Jesus, His presence. My hope is based on my relationship with Jesus throughout the years and days to come. Each day brings an experience of its own. This living hope brings joy. The dark moments are outshined by God's presence and glory. It doesn't matter if I understand it or not. It is not a matter of opinion, but of the heart. My breast cancer experience has been for me a journey to learn more about the One who I love, who I chose to follow and who leads me. Every day is a commitment to praise Him and to seek Him, and to meditate on His blessings. How I react to conflicts, difficult situations and stress, both at work and in personal matters, has changed.

During my journey through breast cancer, my main prayer was:

> *My Lord, give me the understanding to comprehend your Word and to know when you speak to my soul. In receiving you, I receive your life. Show me to understand the purpose of any storm in my life, so that in the middle of it, I could feel the certainty that together with your life, I will experience in growth your renovating power through it. Lord I thank you for the opportunity to affirm your majesty in my life. I ask you the courage to affirm your presence in my circumstances; thus to see your glory in my life, the way you want me to see it.*

I meditated often on these Bible verses:

> *Do not be anxious about anything, but in everything, by prayer and petition, with thanksgiving, present your requests*

to God. And the peace of God, which transcends all understanding, will guard your hearts and your minds in Christ Jesus.
(Philippians 4:6-7, NIV)

Let him lead me to the banquet hall, and let his banner over me be love. . . . His left arm is under my head, and his right arm embraces me.
(Song of Solomon 2:4,6, NIV)

When you pass through the waters, I will be with you; and when you pass through the rivers, they will not sweep over you. When you walk through the fire, you will not be burned; the flames will not set you ablaze.
(Isaiah 43:2, NIV)

But he said to me, "My grace is sufficient for you, for my power is made perfect in weakness." Therefore I will boast all the more gladly about my weaknesses, so that Christ's power may rest on me.
(2 Corinthians 12:9, NIV)

[7]But we have this treasure in jars of clay to show that this all-surpassing power is from God and not from us. [8]We are hard pressed on every side, but not crushed; perplexed, but not in despair; [9]persecuted, but not abandoned; struck down, but not destroyed. [10]We always carry around in our body the death of Jesus, so that the life of Jesus may also be revealed in our body. . . . [16] Therefore we do not lose heart. Though outwardly we are wasting away, yet inwardly we are being renewed day by day. [17]For our light and momentary troubles are achieving for us an eternal glory that far outweighs them all.
(2 Corinthians 4:7-17, NIV)

When I meditate on these verses I'm thankful for the opportunity to affirm the Lord's majesty in my life. It is not that I'm strong on my own, but that the Almighty fills me with strength. I'm humbled to know that I'm His and that He carries me.

A New Stance

When I started sharing my cancer experience, I immediately started getting feedback from people on how my experience was touching them and was inspiring them. I started realizing that my cancer fight was not an isolated event, but a way for God to bring glory to His name in my life, my family and others. I had to share how God was working in my life. God was with me all the way. He was, and is, my provider.

This is my testimony. I cannot be silent. God has given me this time and I will not be idle! To understand that God can use me is an amazing feeling and I cannot take it lightly. I'm a not an accident of the universe. I'm here for a purpose.

God has given me this time and I will not be idle!

Mission Statement

Tragedy and illness, such as cancer, give you a new attitude toward life. I can distinguish more clearly what matters from what is superfluous.

As a parent, I have a mission to my kids and I need to let them know they are important and that I care for them, not only with words but also with deeds. I always strive to be intentional about the time I spend with them. If they feel upset and want to cry about something, I tell them I want to cry with them, too. They give me the "weird look" and then we laugh and look at the situation from a new perspective. I want to show them that if life doesn't smile upon us, we need to persevere and smile at it anyway. I want them to understand that although life is not always easy and bright, we have to stand firm and face our obstacles with confidence, with faith, with the knowledge that we are not alone. We have the hand of God to help us and His light to shine upon us.

Sometimes, soon after my cancer treatment was over, I found myself struggling because I couldn't establish specific goals for my career or personal life, other than to live, to see my kids, and to be a positive influence in others' lives. One day my younger son came back from school with a homework assignment to get together as a family and come up with a family mission statement. He was given a week to complete this task.

A New Stance

I took that homework seriously because at exactly that time in my life I was struggling to find a new goal and a new inspiration. In the process to build the mission statement, we talked about what was important to us in life and what could we do to frame that as a family Mission Statement. We spoke about, "what was important for us?" and, "what are we going to do about it?" After a couple of drafts, adjustments and a family vote, this is the final version that we came up with:

> Family Mission Statement
> To make a difference in the world by sowing love,
> to keep our focus in Jesus by listening to Him
> and growing in His knowledge, and to share our joy.
> So that we can say at the end of the day,
> that we touched others and bore good fruits.

Our Mission Statement is posted on our refrigerator door so we can see it every day. Yes, I do want world peace and harmony, too, so my resolution is to sow these in my immediate family and those within my reach. Sow peace and harmony with love and pray for that seed to grow. It is not about the struggles that you may encounter, but about what you can do to overcome them.

Use Your Energy Wisely

Gossip, anger and hate are not worth the energy. One day someone at work tried to make me angry and upset saying stupid things just to get my attention. I just waved to him and prayed for him. Later, he asked me if I would ever get angry and challenged me to show him my anger using sarcasm. I told him that I was not going to waste my valued energy on anger; it was not worth it. I added that I was just given a second chance at life and that I took that very seriously. I just couldn't waste my precious energy on anger or cultivating bitterness and grudges. There was nothing he could say to that. He just stared at me. After that I think he saw me as an alien from another planet, but I earned his respect. Don't waste your precious energy cultivating bitterness or anger that is not productive. Try instead to

Of course I can get angry sometimes, but I'm careful to not waste that energy on something that doesn't really matter. Even on that I'm very selective.

focus on action instead of reaction. Of course I can get angry sometimes, but I'm careful to not waste that energy on something that doesn't really matter. Even on that I'm very selective.

I've learned to listen and to choose my words carefully. One day at church, Pastor Sean Azzaro said: "Words are easy to throw around but impossible to take them back." Certainly it is so.

> *Everyone should be quick to listen, slow to speak and slow to become angry . . .*
> *(James 1:19, NIV)*

I want my kids to understand that they don't have to prove anything to anyone. I want them to know that God knows their heart and they have to keep faithful to their mission. I want everyone to understand that God is not just someone to turn to when going through rough times. He is always there, in every moment. I used to think that it was very important to me to be independent, but that has changed. It's amazing to realize that I'm depending on God. I cannot speak about myself and leave God out of the picture.

Marked for Life

I cannot go on in life pretending that the cancer is something in the past, that nothing has happened and go back to my old routine. I'm not only physically marked, but also emotionally and spiritually marked. I have a "new normal" now. Every fiber within me has changed. After the cancer, I see life through different eyes now. Big goals seem trivial and everyday trivial things are magical. Things I never did before, such as waking up early to eat breakfast in bed with Angel and spend some time together before waking up the kids and going to work, are things I now treasure.

I also find myself many times staring at my kids for no reason. If they are doing homework I just sit there at the table with them, waiting for them to ask me questions. Just looking at them and paying attention to them is a great blessing; a blessing that cannot be underestimated. I'm witnessing their lives, and for that, I am grateful.

When I look my kids, I see who they are and how they are transforming before my eyes. I'm witnessing two wonderful lives being molded and growing . . . and I feel a deep respect toward the mission that God gave me for them. I cannot take them for granted. They are not my possessions, but blessings. My mission is to love them, to educate them, to be there for them, to inspire them, to teach them, to lead them, and most of all, to share with them the greatest gift of all: the magnificent presence of the Lord, His love and His Word. When I see my boys, I see the plan that God has for them. I see a purpose in each of them. And is my duty to guide them and pray each day for direction to shepherd them, so that they keep seeking the Lord and establish a relationship with Him so that the truth of His Word is revealed to them.

No Instruction Manual?

When my kids tell me, "Mom, I love you;" I don't know if they have any idea of how much that means to me. I love to see how much they love each other and how they express that love among themselves. At home we have a rule that if anybody is upset at someone, we establish clearly that we love each other even if we are upset. If I'm upset for something they did, I communicate the reason to them and make them understand that if I get upset it is because I care for them and love them.

I try to let them understand that I will be there for them as long as God allows me to be. I want them to understand that even if they make a mistake my love toward them is bigger. Of course I expect God to grant me the wisdom to help them understand that sometimes our mistakes can have consequences. I tell them that I seek the love of God to act with wisdom and not rebuke them in anger. I always tell them that mistakes are great learning opportunities.

The same can apply when facing changes. No one can live enough with a crippling fear of making mistakes, stumbling or in fear of change that would prevent one from embracing new opportunities and learning. Understand that faith in not just something to practice in church, but an everyday part of our lives. If I want my children to learn this, I have to set the example.

It is well known that children come into this world without an instruction manual. Similarly, people enter into relationships with many assumptions and without instruction manuals. On the other hand, I also know that when King Solomon started his reign, God asked Solomon to choose anything he wanted for Him to give it to him and Solomon chose wisdom to guide their people (2 Chronicles 1:7-10). Therefore, I cannot do less than that. I constantly ask God for wisdom and direction to lead my children and to manage my family affairs. Again, I cannot talk about me and my family and leave God out of the picture. I cannot separate my essence from who I am.

> *[7] That night God appeared to Solomon and said to him, "Ask for whatever you want me to give you." . . . [10] Give me wisdom and knowledge, that I may lead this people, for who is able to govern this great people of yours?*
> *(2 Chronicles 1:7-10, NIV)*

> *[5] If any of you lacks wisdom, you should ask God, who gives generously to all without finding fault, and it will be given to you. [6] But when you ask, you must believe and not doubt, because the one who doubts is like a wave of the sea, blown and tossed by the wind. [7] That person should not expect to receive anything from the Lord. [8] Such a person is double-minded and unstable in all they do.*
> *(James 1:5-8, NIV)*

> *The fear of the Lord is the beginning of wisdom; . . .*
> *(Psalms 111:10, NIV)*

Neither do I have an instruction manual, but I do have the Word of God. As a matter of life and death I cannot be silent about seeing and experiencing God's power and intervention in my life. This is my testimony. The time I have is <u>now</u> and I'm not going to be passive. It all starts with just one step. Come and see!

The Five W's

How many times we have approached to God in prayer with this mind set?—"I want what I want when I want it!" How many times has this behavior has impacted our relationship with God? We are so focused on what we want and when we want it. We tell God what we think we need and as time passes and we don't see any hint or response, we get disappointed or angry. We may think: "God didn't hear me" or "God didn't give me what I needed." As result, we distance ourselves from the One who loves us and can redeem us.

When I faced the reality that I had breast cancer, I was tempted so many times to pray like that. I knew that God loved me and that He knew my heart and that He is merciful. I was so tempted to ask Him to get that cancer out of my body "now" (or "soon," to try to be humble) so I could testify that He healed me. Note that I say I was tempted, but refrained myself from praying like that. I could feel that God had something bigger that He wanted me to focus on. He wanted me to focus on the journey and not the way out. He wanted me to focus on His glory and not on what I thought I needed or what I thought was convenient. My prayer was instead, "Show me," "Let me feel your presence," "Guide me through this," "Prepare me to feel your glory," "Hold my hand," "Shine," "This is for Your glory!" I realized I didn't have to get what I think I needed to testify, but that I could testify, even in the middle of the storm, about witnessing His presence, love and hope in the midst of uncertainty. It was not about me, but about what He wanted to do through me. It was about His glory.

> *I could feel that God had something bigger that He wanted me to focus on. He wanted me to focus on the journey and not the way out. He wanted me to focus on His glory and not on what I thought I needed or what I thought was convenient.*

> *"For my thoughts are not your thoughts, neither are your ways my ways," declares the Lord. "As the heavens are higher than the earth, so are my ways higher than your ways, and my thoughts than your thoughts.*
> *(Isaiah 55:8-9, NIV)*

The Five W's

I had to hold high my faith in spite of some people who looked at me as if I did something wrong in my spiritual life and I was paying for it, or made me feel that I was not filled enough with the Holy Spirit. I also knew that there were many of people praying for me in many different ways. I experienced joy because I knew that God was hearing these prayers. Life is too precious and we cannot waste it living in fear or with a bitter heart. Life is short. I was experiencing so many blessings that I felt I had to share them with others.

It was not about waiting to figure things out to be able to share my blessings, but about sharing my blessings regardless of the circumstances. I had to make the journey of confiding in the Lord my weakness, growing in His knowledge, serving others, engaging in doing, living to show my kids not to live in fear or despair, but in trust and faith no matter the circumstances around us. I had the urgency to show my kids, at their young age, that it is not our circumstances that define us, but the way how we face and endure our circumstances. God's love and the real life through Jesus is my precious gift. I have to offer that to my boys—and to anyone—with the time I have.

Yes, I was so tempted to pray, "I want what I want when I want it!" I am so glad I didn't. Because although I know that God took care of my cancer, He also showed me something bigger: He gave me his hand, He showed me his loving care, He carried me, He let me experience His Word, He let me feel how He was fighting my battles with me, He led me with shining light, He inundated me with His presence, He let me experience a more closer relationship with Him, He guided me to a precious bonding with my husband and kids. That experience helped me to feel His glory in me and around me. I now see life with different eyes. Life is short and there is so much to do.

> *I will bring the blind by a way they did not know;*
> *I will lead them in paths they have not known.*
> *I will make darkness light before them,*
> *And crooked places straight.*
> *These things I will do for them,*
> *And not forsake them.*
> *(Isaiah 42:16, NKJV)*

If you have been in the 5 "W's" or are stuck in them, it's okay; it's not the end. It's just a matter of choosing to move on and change behavior. God has promised to guide us—even in prayer—so let Him.

The Prayers

I started writing this book to describe my journey through cancer. Later I realized that my story goes beyond my cancer battle. It is my hope that anybody facing any struggle or questions about life can find courage and inspiration throughout this book, throughout my own prayers.

Here are some prayers I poured out from my heart during my journey:

Journal Entry

Today I prayed with Alejandro:

"Dear Lord, we are in your hands. We know that if you tell this cancer to go away and disappear, the cancer will go away. Meanwhile, may your name be glorified in this situation, in our lives. Help the unbeliever to believe that you are the God Almighty. We are in your hands. Guide us in our faith. In Jesus name, amen."

Journal Entry

This is the confidence we have in approaching God: that if we ask anything according to his will, he hears us. And if we know that he hears us—whatever we ask—we know that we have what we asked of him.
(1 John 5:14-15, NIV)

Oh Lord, help me pray in your will . . .

Journal Entry

About prayer, I have learned a lot this year. I don't know where to begin to describe how wonderful God has been with me. How He has guided me and the things He had revealed me. How he has loved me and hugged me. His hand has transcended even more of what I would have imagined.

Oh God, you know all things. Lord, I give you this heart, knowing with all certainty, that you know what is best for me. I acknowledge that the key for your great blessing is to have a well-disposed heart. Lord, here I am.

Journal Entry

Then you will call, and the LORD will answer; you will cry for help,
and he will say: Here am I . . .
(Isaiah 58:9, NIV)

Thank you Lord for the certainty of your presence. Guard my heart and my mind from anxiety . . . lead my steps.

Journal Entry

[4] Let him lead me to the banquet hall, and let his banner over me be love.
[6] His left arm is under my head, and his right arm embraces me.
(Song of Solomon 2:4,6, NIV)

Thank you Lord because even if I feel insufficient, frustrated and/or overwhelmed by my circumstances, your love snuggles me, feeds me and heartens me.

Journal Entry

⁷ But we have this treasure in jars of clay to show that this all-surpassing power is from God and not from us. ⁸ We are hard pressed on every side, but not crushed; perplexed, but not in despair; ⁹ persecuted, but not abandoned; struck down, but not destroyed. ¹⁰ We always carry around in our body the death of Jesus, so that the life of Jesus may also be revealed in our body. . . . ¹⁶ Therefore we do not lose heart. Though outwardly we are wasting away, yet inwardly we are being renewed day by day.
¹⁷ For our light and momentary troubles are achieving for us an eternal glory that far outweighs them all.
(2 Corinthians 4:7-17, NIV)

My Lord, give me understanding to comprehend your Word and to know when you speak to my soul. In receiving you, I receive your life. Show me to understand the purpose of any storm or harsh wind in my life, so that instead of avoiding it, I decide to carry with joy the certainty that together with your life, I will experience in growth your renovating power through it. Lord I thank you for the opportunity to affirm your majesty in my life. I ask you the courage to affirm your presence in my circumstances; thus to see your glory in my life, the way you want me to see it.

Journal Entry

There is no moment in my life, Oh God, which I couldn't find you; in every sadness and in the joy. There is no distance that could join us or that could separate us. Oh God you truly ARE. Your presence is beyond my understanding. Your love is everlasting.

The Prayers

Journal Entry

When you pass through the waters, I will be with you; and when you pass through the rivers, they will not sweep over you. When you walk through the fire, you will not be burned; the flames will not set you ablaze.
(Isaiah 43:2, NIV)

If there is a storm surrounding me, Lord, show me your peace and sustain me in it.

Journal Entry

My exhaustion and praise are yours . . . I don't have anything to offer you, only my heart marked by your love and the joy of the blessings that you have already given me. All I am, indeed, is yours.

Journal Entry

Dear Lord, may all that do not know you, understand that you are not a religion, nor an image, nor a portrait of our minds. May them understand that you are our Creator, that you are love, life above all. May them be embraced by your loving Spirit, by the reality of your presence. May them see and experience your reality. May them understand your voice.

*O LORD, revive Your work in the midst of the years!
In the midst of the years make it known; . . .*
(Habakkuk 3:2, NKJV)

The Sword

> [16] *In addition to all this, take up the shield of faith, with which you can extinguish all the flaming arrows of the evil one.*
> [17] *. . . and the sword of the Spirit, which is the word of God.*
> [18] *And pray in the Spirit on all occasions with all kinds of prayers . .*
> *(Ephesians 6:16-18, NIV)*

The sword, the Word of God, can be an useful tool to inspire you, but it is not only about inspiration. A warrior also needs a shield or else his or her armor is incomplete. The shield is faith. The faith is up to you. I'm not talking about a religious faith or positivism. It is the faith as described in the book of Hebrews:

> *Now faith is the assurance of things hoped for, the conviction of things not seen.*
> *(Hebrews 11:1, ESV)*

> *And without faith it is impossible to please God, because anyone who comes to him must believe that he exists and that he rewards those who earnestly seek him.*
> *(Hebrews 11:6, NIV)*

> *Then Jesus said, "Did I not tell you that if you believe, you will see the glory of God?"*
> *(John 11:40, NIV)*

In my battle with breast cancer, faith was my shield, the Word of God my sword and prayer was my food. The Word of God speaks . . .

> *For the word of God is alive and active. . . .*
> *(Hebrews 4:12, NIV)*

I've grouped the various Bible verses that gave me hope throughout my battle according to the specific need I had and depending on the situation I was facing. May the Word of God speak to you as it does for me.

The Sword

Need Strength?

Joshua 1:9, NKJV: Be strong and of good courage; do not be afraid, nor be dismayed, for the LORD your God is with you wherever you go.

2 Corinthians 12:9, NIV: But he said to me, "My grace is sufficient for you, for my power is made perfect in weakness." Therefore I will boast all the more gladly about my weaknesses, so that Christ's power may rest on me.

Psalms 63:7-8, NIV: Because you are my help, I sing in the shadow of your wings. I cling to you; your right hand upholds me.

Psalms 27:3, NIV: Though an army besiege me, my heart will not fear; though war break out against me, even then I will be confident.

Psalms 23:2-3, NIV: He makes me lie down in green pastures, he leads me beside quiet waters, he refreshes my soul. He guides me along the right paths for his name's sake.

Isaiah 41:10, NIV: So do not fear, for I am with you; do not be dismayed, for I am your God. I will strengthen you and help you; I will uphold you with my righteous right hand.

2 Corinthians 4:7-17, NIV: [7] But we have this treasure in jars of clay to show that this all-surpassing power is from God and not from us. [8] We are hard pressed on every side, but not crushed; perplexed, but not in despair; [9] persecuted, but not abandoned; struck down, but not destroyed. [10] We always carry around in our body the death of Jesus, so that the life of Jesus may also be revealed in our body. . . . [16] Therefore we do not lose heart. Though outwardly we are wasting away, yet inwardly we are being renewed day by day. [17] For our light and momentary troubles are achieving for us an eternal glory that far outweighs them all.

Song of Solomon 2:4-6, NIV: Let him lead me to the banquet hall, and let his banner over me be love. . . . His left arm is under my head, and his right arm embraces me.

Isaiah 43:2, NIV: When you pass through the waters, I will be with you; and when you pass through the rivers, they will not sweep over you. When you walk through the fire, you will not be burned; the flames will not set you ablaze.

Need Direction?

Luke 8:50, NKJV: "Do not be afraid; only believe, . . .

COURAGE UNDER FIRE

Psalms 5:3, NIV: In the morning, LORD, you hear my voice; in the morning I lay my requests before you and wait expectantly.

Jeremiah 33:3, NIV: Call to me and I will answer you and tell you great and unsearchable things you do not know.

Isaiah 58:10-11, NCV: [10] if you feed those who are hungry and take care of the needs of those who are troubled, then your light will shine in the darkness, and you will be bright like sunshine at noon. [11] The Lord will always lead you. He will satisfy your needs in dry lands and give strength to your bones. You will be like a garden that has much water, like a spring that never runs dry.

Psalms 119:105, NIV: Your word is a lamp to my feet and a light for my path.

Proverbs 1:23, NKJV: Surely I will pour out my spirit on you; I will make my words known to you.

Battling Anxiety or Uncertainty?

1 Peter 5:7, NIV: Cast all your anxiety on him because he cares for you.

Psalms 42:5, NIV: [5] Why are you downcast, O my soul? Why so disturbed within me? Put your hope in God, for I will yet praise him, my Savior and my God.

Psalms 27:3, NIV: Though an army besiege me, my heart will not fear; though war break out against me, even then I will be confident.

Psalms 42:8, KJV: By day the Lord directs his love, at night his song is with me—a prayer to the God of my life.

Mathew 6:31-34, NIV: [31]So do not worry, saying, "What shall we eat?" or "What shall we drink?" or "What shall we wear?" [32] . . . your heavenly Father knows that you need them. [33]But seek first his kingdom and his righteousness, and all these things will be given to you as well. [34]Therefore do not worry about tomorrow, . . .
Philippians 4:6-7, NIV: Do not be anxious about anything, but in everything, by prayer and petition, with thanksgiving, present your requests to God. And the peace of God, which transcends all understanding, will guard your hearts and your minds in Christ Jesus.

Isaiah 41:13, NIV: For I am the LORD, your God, who takes hold of your right hand and says to you, Do not fear; I will help you.

Luke 8:50, NKJV: "Do not be afraid; only believe, . . .

The Sword

Psalms 121, NIV: [1] I lift up my eyes to the mountains— where does my help come from? [2] My help comes from the Lord, the Maker of heaven and earth... (Continue reading the whole Psalm)

Mathew 6:26, NKJV: Look at the birds of the air, for they neither sow nor reap nor gather into barns; yet your heavenly Father feeds them. Are you not of more value than they?

2 Corinthians 4:7-17, NIV: [7] But we have this treasure in jars of clay to show that this all-surpassing power is from God and not from us. [8] We are hard pressed on every side, but not crushed; perplexed, but not in despair; [9] persecuted, but not abandoned; struck down, but not destroyed. [10] We always carry around in our body the death of Jesus, so that the life of Jesus may also be revealed in our body. . . . [16] Therefore we do not lose heart. Though outwardly we are wasting away, yet inwardly we are being renewed day by day. [17] For our light and momentary troubles are achieving for us an eternal glory that far outweighs them all.

Isaiah 26:3-4, NCV: [3] You, Lord, give true peace to those who depend on you, because they trust you. [4] So, trust the Lord always, because he is our Rock forever.

Battling Fear?

Joshua 1:9, NKJV: Be strong and of good courage; do not be afraid, nor be dismayed, for the LORD your God is with you wherever you go."

Luke 8:50, NKJV: "Do not be afraid; only believe, . . .

Psalms 56:3, NKJV : Whenever I am afraid, I will trust in You.

Psalms 91:4, NIV: He will cover you with his feathers, and under his wings you will find refuge; his faithfulness will be your shield and rampart.

Psalms 27:3, NIV: Though an army besiege me, my heart will not fear; though war break out against me, even then I will be confident.

Jeremiah 20:11, NIV: But the Lord is with me like a mighty warrior; . . .

Isaiah 41:13, NIV: For I am the LORD, your God, who takes hold of your right hand and says to you, Do not fear; I will help you.

Isaiah 41:10, NIV: So do not fear, for I am with you; do not be dismayed, for I am your God. I will strengthen you and help you; I will uphold you with my righteous right hand.

Psalms 23, NIV: [1] The Lord is my shepherd, I lack nothing. [2] He makes me lie down in green pastures, he leads me beside quiet waters,... (Continue reading the whole Psalm)

Isaiah 58:9, NIV: Then you will call, and the LORD will answer; you will cry for help, and he will say: Here am I...

Isaiah 43:2, NIV: When you pass through the waters, I will be with you; and when you pass through the rivers, they will not sweep over you. When you walk through the fire, you will not be burned; the flames will not set you ablaze.

Need Confirmation of God's Promises?

2 Corinthians 1:20-22, NKJV: For all the promises of God in Him are Yes, and in Him Amen, to the glory of God through us. Now He who establishes us with you in Christ and has anointed us is God, who also has sealed us and given us the Spirit in our hearts as a guarantee.

Psalms 42:8, KJV: By day the Lord directs his love, at night his song is with me— a prayer to the God of my life.

2 Peter 1:3-4, NIV: His divine power has given us everything we need for life and godliness through our knowledge of him who called us by his own glory and goodness. Through these he has given us his very great and precious promises, so that through them you may participate in the divine nature and escape the corruption in the world caused by evil desires.

Isaiah 55:8-11, NIV: [8] 'For my thoughts are not your thoughts, neither are your ways my ways,' declares the LORD. [9] "As the heavens are higher than the earth, so are my ways higher than your ways and my thoughts than your thoughts. [10] As the rain and the snow come down from heaven, and do not return to it without watering the earth and making it bud and flourish, so that it yields seed for the sower and bread for the eater, [11] so is my word that goes out from my mouth: It will not return to me empty, but will accomplish what I desire and achieve the purpose for which I sent it.

Need Hope?

Jeremiah 29:11-12, NIV: For I know the plans I have for you," declares the LORD, "plans to prosper you and not to harm you, plans to give you hope and a future. Then you will call on me and come and pray to me, and I will listen to you.

2 Corinthians 4:17, NIV: For our light and momentary troubles are achieving for us an eternal glory that far outweighs them all.

The Sword

2 Corinthians 12:9, NIV: But he said to me, 'My grace is sufficient for you, for my power is made perfect in weakness.' Therefore I will boast all the more gladly about my weaknesses, so that Christ's power may rest on me.

Isaiah 58:10-11, NCV : [10] if you feed those who are hungry and take care of the needs of those who are troubled, then your light will shine in the darkness, and you will be bright like sunshine at noon. [11] The Lord will always lead you. He will satisfy your needs in dry lands and give strength to your bones. You will be like a garden that has much water, like a spring that never runs dry.

Jeremiah 33:3, NIV: Call to me and I will answer you and tell you great and unsearchable things you do not know.

2 Corinthians 4:7-17, NIV: [7] But we have this treasure in jars of clay to show that this all-surpassing power is from God and not from us. [8] We are hard pressed on every side, but not crushed; perplexed, but not in despair; [9] persecuted, but not abandoned; struck down, but not destroyed. [10] We always carry around in our body the death of Jesus, so that the life of Jesus may also be revealed in our body. . . . [16] Therefore we do not lose heart. Though outwardly we are wasting away, yet inwardly we are being renewed day by day. [17] For our light and momentary troubles are achieving for us an eternal glory that far outweighs them all.

Isaiah 42:16, NKJV: I will lead the blind by ways they have not known, along unfamiliar paths I will guide them; I will turn the darkness into light before them and make the rough places smooth. These are the things I will do; I will not forsake them.

2 Corinthians 4:16-18, NIV: [16] Therefore we do not lose heart. Though outwardly we are wasting away, yet inwardly we are being renewed day by day. [17] For our light and momentary troubles are achieving for us an eternal glory that far outweighs them all. [18] So we fix our eyes not on what is seen, but on what is unseen, since what is seen is temporary, but what is unseen is eternal.

1 Peter 1:3-9 (NLT): [3] All praise to God, the Father of our Lord Jesus Christ. It is by his great mercy that we have been born again, because God raised Jesus Christ from the dead. Now we live with great expectation, [4] and we have a priceless inheritance—an inheritance that is kept in heaven for you, pure and undefiled, beyond the reach of change and decay. [5] And through your faith, God is protecting you by his power until you receive this salvation, which is ready to be revealed on the last day for all to see. [6] So be truly glad. There is wonderful joy ahead, even though you have to endure many trials for a little while. [7] These trials will show that your faith is genuine. It is being tested as fire tests and purifies gold—though your faith is far more precious than mere gold. So when your faith remains strong through many trials, it will bring you much praise and glory and honor on the day when Jesus Christ is revealed to the whole world. [8] You love him even though you have never seen him. Though you do

not see him now, you trust him; and you rejoice with a glorious, inexpressible joy. ⁹ The reward for trusting him will be the salvation of your souls.

Need Faith?

Hebrews 11:1, NIV: Now faith is confidence in what we hope for and assurance about what we do not see.

2 Corinthians 4:7-17, NIV: ⁷ But we have this treasure in jars of clay to show that this all-surpassing power is from God and not from us. ⁸ We are hard pressed on every side, but not crushed; perplexed, but not in despair; ⁹ persecuted, but not abandoned; struck down, but not destroyed. ¹⁰ We always carry around in our body the death of Jesus, so that the life of Jesus may also be revealed in our body. . . . ¹⁶ Therefore we do not lose heart. Though outwardly we are wasting away, yet inwardly we are being renewed day by day. ¹⁷ For our light and momentary troubles are achieving for us an eternal glory that far outweighs them all.

Mathew 14:22-33, NIV: ²² Immediately Jesus made the disciples get into the boat and go on ahead of him to the other side, while he dismissed the crowd. . . . ²⁴ and the boat was already a considerable distance from land, buffeted by the waves because the wind was against it. ²⁵ During the fourth watch of the night Jesus went out to them, walking on the lake. ²⁶ When the disciples saw him walking on the lake, they were terrified. "It's a ghost," they said, and cried out in fear. ²⁷ But Jesus immediately said to them: "Take courage! It is I. Don't be afraid." ²⁸ "Lord, if it's you," Peter replied, "tell me to come to you on the water." ²⁹ "Come," he said. Then Peter got down out of the boat, walked on the water and came toward Jesus. ³⁰ But when he saw the wind, he was afraid and, beginning to sink, cried out, "Lord, save me!" ³¹ Immediately Jesus reached out his hand and caught him. "You of little faith," he said, "why did you doubt?" ³² And when they climbed into the boat, the wind died down. ³³ Then those who were in the boat worshiped him, saying, "Truly you are the Son of God."

Mark 9:23-24, NIV: "If you can?" said Jesus. "Everything is possible for him who believes." Immediately the boy's father exclaimed, "I do believe; help me overcome my unbelief!"

Matthew 9:22, NIV: Jesus turned and saw her. "Take heart, daughter," he said, "your faith has healed you." And the woman was healed at that moment.

Mark 10:52, NIV: "Go," said Jesus, "your faith has healed you." Immediately he received his sight and followed Jesus along the road.

John 11:40, NIV: Then Jesus said, "Did I not tell you that if you believe, you will see the glory of God?"

Isaiah 26:3-4, NCV: ³ You, Lord, give true peace to those who depend on you, because they trust you. ⁴ So, trust the Lord always, because he is our Rock forever.

2 Corinthians 1:20-22, NKJV: For all the promises of God in Him are Yes, and in Him Amen, to the glory of God through us. Now He who establishes us with you in Christ and has anointed us is God, who also has sealed us and given us the Spirit in our hearts as a guarantee.

2 Peter 1:3-4, NIV: His divine power has given us everything we need for life and godliness through our knowledge of him who called us by his own glory and goodness. Through these he has given us his very great and precious promises, so that through them you may participate in the divine nature and escape the corruption in the world caused by evil desires.

James 1:2-7, NIV: ² Consider it pure joy, my brothers and sisters, whenever you face trials of many kinds, ³ because you know that the testing of your faith produces perseverance. ⁴ Let perseverance finish its work so that you may be mature and complete, not lacking anything. ⁵ If any of you lacks wisdom, you should ask God, who gives generously to all without finding fault, and it will be given to you. ⁶ But when you ask, you must believe and not doubt, because the one who doubts is like a wave of the sea, blown and tossed by the wind. ⁷ That person should not expect to receive anything from the Lord.

Need Joy?

1 Peter 1:3-9 (NLT): ³ All praise to God, the Father of our Lord Jesus Christ. It is by his great mercy that we have been born again, because God raised Jesus Christ from the dead. Now we live with great expectation, ⁴ and we have a priceless inheritance—an inheritance that is kept in heaven for you, pure and undefiled, beyond the reach of change and decay. ⁵ And through your faith, God is protecting you by his power until you receive this salvation, which is ready to be revealed on the last day for all to see. ⁶ So be truly glad. There is wonderful joy ahead, even though you have to endure many trials for a little while. ⁷ These trials will show that your faith is genuine. It is being tested as fire tests and purifies gold—though your faith is far more precious than mere gold. So when your faith remains strong through many trials, it will bring you much praise and glory and honor on the day when Jesus Christ is revealed to the whole world. ⁸ You love him even though you have never seen him. Though you do not see him now, you trust him; and you rejoice with a glorious, inexpressible joy. ⁹ The reward for trusting him will be the salvation of your souls.

James 1:2-7, NIV: ² Consider it pure joy, my brothers and sisters, whenever you face trials of many kinds, ³ because you know that the testing of your faith produces perseverance. ⁴ Let perseverance finish its work so that you may be mature and complete, not lacking anything. ⁵ If any of you lacks wisdom, you should ask God, who gives generously to all without finding fault, and it will be given to you. ⁶ But when you ask, you must believe and not doubt, because the one who doubts is like a wave of the sea, blown and tossed by the wind. ⁷ That person should not expect to receive anything from the Lord.

Psalms 37:4, NIV: Take delight in the Lord, and he will give you the desires of your heart.

John 15:8-11, NIV: ⁸ This is to my Father's glory, that you bear much fruit, showing yourselves to be my disciples. ⁹ "As the Father has loved me, so have I loved you. Now remain in my love. ¹⁰ If you keep my commands, you will remain in my love, just as I have kept my Father's commands and remain in his love. ¹¹ I have told you this so that my joy may be in you and that your joy may be complete.

Psalms 16:11, NIV: You make known to me the path of life; you will fill me with joy in your presence, with eternal pleasures at your right hand.

Psalms 51:12, NIV: Restore to me the joy of your salvation and grant me a willing spirit, to sustain me.

Psalms 51:8, NIV: Let me hear joy and gladness; let the bones you have crushed rejoice.

Psalms 119:111, NIV: Your statutes are my heritage forever; they are the joy of my heart.

Romans 12:12, NIV: Be joyful in hope, patient in affliction, faithful in prayer.

Romans 15:13, NIV: May the God of hope fill you with all joy and peace as you trust in him, so that you may overflow with hope by the power of the Holy Spirit.

2 Corinthians 12:10, NIV: That is why, for Christ's sake, I delight in weaknesses, in insults, in hardships, in persecutions, in difficulties. For when I am weak, then I am strong.

John 16:21-22, NIV: ²¹ A woman giving birth to a child has pain because her time has come; but when her baby is born she forgets the anguish because of her joy that a child is born into the world. ²² So with you: Now is your time of grief, but I will see you again and you will rejoice, and no one will take away your joy.

The Sword

In Prayer?

Ephesians 3:20, NKJV: Now to Him who is able to do exceedingly abundantly above all that we ask or think, according to the power that works in us,

Psalms 42:8, KJV: By day the Lord directs his love, at night his song is with me—a prayer to the God of my life.

Isaiah 58:9, NIV: Then you will call, and the LORD will answer; you will cry for help, and he will say: Here am I...

1 Samuel 3:9 (NIV): 'Speak, Lord, for your servant is listening.' . . .

Philippians 4:6-7, NIV: [6] Do not be anxious about anything, but in every situation, by prayer and petition, with thanksgiving, present your requests to God. [7] And the peace of God, which transcends all understanding, will guard your hearts and your minds in Christ Jesus.

Mark 12:30, NIV: Love the Lord your God with all your heart and with all your soul and with all your mind and with all your strength.

Revelation 3:20, NIV: Here I am! I stand at the door and knock. If anyone hears my voice and opens the door, I will come in and eat with him, and he with me.

1 John 5:14-15, NIV: This is the confidence we have in approaching God: that if we ask anything according to his will, he hears us. And if we know that he hears us—whatever we ask—we know that we have what we asked of him.

Psalms 145:18, ESV: The LORD is near to all who call on him, to all who call on him in truth.

Romans 8:26, NIV: In the same way, the Spirit helps us in our weakness. We do not know what we ought to pray for, but the Spirit himself intercedes for us through wordless groans.

James 1:5-7, NIV: [5] If any of you lacks wisdom, you should ask God, who gives generously to all without finding fault, and it will be given to you. [6] But when you ask, you must believe and not doubt, because the one who doubts is like a wave of the sea, blown and tossed by the wind. [7] That person should not expect to receive anything from the Lord.

Psalms 30:11-12, NIV: You turned my wailing into dancing; you removed my sackcloth and clothed me with joy, that my heart may sing your praises and not be silent. LORD my God, I will praise you forever.

Ephesians 6:18, NIV: And pray in the Spirit on all occasions with all kinds of prayers and requests. With this in mind, be alert and always keep on praying for all the Lord's people.

Mark 9:24, NKJV: "Lord, I believe; help my unbelief!"

Psalms 145:18, ESV: The Lord is near to all who call on him, to all who call on him in truth.

The Sword

In the morning, LORD, you hear my voice;
in the morning I lay my requests before you and wait expectantly.
(Psalms 5:3, NIV)

"Since I play the violin, I saw myself as the violin and the Lord as the master violinist who was refurbishing and tuning the instrument with so much love and tenderness, for that violin to make a beautiful sound, a wonderful melody in His hands. I couldn't be more honored!"—Yilda

NOTES

A Routine Mammogram
1. Calcifications: Deposits of calcium in the tissues. Calcification in the breast can be seen on a mammogram, but cannot be detected by touch. There are two types of breast calcification, macrocalcification and microcalcification. Macrocalcifications are large deposits and are usually not related to cancer. Microcalcifications are specks of calcium that may be found in an area of rapidly dividing cells. Many microcalcifications clustered together may be a sign of cancer.
(Reference: National Cancer Institute; http://www.cancer.gov/cancertopics/screening/understanding-breast-changes/page6)
Depending on how many calcifications you have, their size, and where they are found, your doctor may ask you to have: Another mammogram, an ultrasound or a biopsy to check for signs of disease.
2. Fibrocystic breasts: A common condition marked by benign (not cancer) changes in breast tissue. These changes may include irregular lumps or cysts, breast discomfort, sensitive nipples, and itching. These symptoms may change throughout the menstrual cycle and usually stop after menopause. Also called benign breast disease, fibrocystic breast changes, and mammary dysplasia.
(Reference: National Cancer Institute; http://www.cancer.gov/dictionary?cdrid=407764)

Sharing the News with Friends and Family
1. Cancer staging: As per the National Cancer Institute (web address: http://www.cancer.gov/cancertopics/factsheet/detection/staging) the key points of cancer staging are:
    a. Staging describes the extent or severity of a person's cancer. Knowing the stage of disease helps the doctor plan treatment and estimate the person's prognosis.
    b. Staging systems for cancer have evolved over time and continue to change as scientists learn more about cancer.
    c. Physical exams, imaging procedures, laboratory tests, pathology reports, and surgical reports provide information to determine the stage of the cancer.
2. "K-LOVE": K-LOVE is a Christian radio station and ministry with the vision to communicate the Gospel through mass media. K-LOVE is a network of contemporary Christian stations using the same identification. K-LOVE was chosen because the "K" indicates it is a radio network that originated west of the Mississippi River. The

NOTES

"LOVE" portion of the name indicates the message of God's love and forgiveness available for all. It is headquartered in Rocklin, CA. The website is "http://www.klove.com"

The Crossroad
1. Lumpectomy: Lumpectomy is also known as breast conserving surgery. It removes only the breast lump and a surrounding margin of normal tissue. Radiation therapy is usually given after a lumpectomy. The main advantage of breast-conserving surgery (BCS) is that a woman keeps most of her breast. A disadvantage is the usual need for radiation therapy—most often for 5 to 6 weeks—after surgery. (Reference: American Cancer Society; http://www.cancer.org/cancer/breastcancer/detailedguide/breast-cancer-treating-surgery)
2. Pathology: Tissue removed during a biopsy is sent to a pathology laboratory, where it is sliced into thin sections for viewing under a microscope. A pathology report is a document that contains the diagnosis determined by examining cells and tissues. The pathologist sends a pathology report to the doctor within 10 days after the biopsy or surgery is performed. Pathology reports are written in technical medical language. The pathology report will provide the size and description of the cancer, how it compares with normal cells, how quickly the tumor is likely to grow and spread and whether hormones or genetic mutations are factors in the cancer's growth. (Reference: National Cancer Institute; http://www.cancer.gov/cancertopics/factsheet/detection/pathology-reports)
3. Cancer Staging: As per the National Cancer Institute, web address: "http://www.cancer.gov/cancertopics/factsheet/detection/staging" the key points of cancer staging are:
    a. Staging describes the extent or severity of a person's cancer. Knowing the stage of disease helps the doctor plan treatment and estimate the person's prognosis.
    b. Staging systems for cancer have evolved over time and continue to change as scientists learn more about cancer.
    c. Physical exams, imaging procedures, laboratory tests, pathology reports, and surgical reports provide information to determine the stage of the cancer.
4. Margins: The edge or border of the tissue removed in cancer surgery. The margin is described as negative or clean when the pathologist finds no cancer cells at the edge of the tissue, suggesting that all of the cancer has been removed. The margin is described as positive or involved when the pathologist finds cancer cells at the edge of the tissue, suggesting that all of the cancer has not been

NOTES

removed. (Reference: National Cancer Institute; http://www.cancer.gov/dictionary?cdrid=44531)

5. Mastectomy: Surgery to remove part or all of the breast. There are different types of mastectomy that differ in the amount of tissue and lymph nodes removed. (Reference: National Cancer Institute; http://en.wikipedia.org/wiki/Mastectomy)
6. Metastasized: To spread from one part of the body to another. When cancer cells metastasize and form secondary tumors, the cells in the metastatic tumor are like those in the original (primary) tumor.
(Reference: http://www.cancer.gov/Common/PopUps/popDefinition.aspx?term=metastasize&version=Patient&language=English)
7. Sentinel lymph node biopsy: A sentinel lymph node biopsy (SLNB) is a procedure in which the sentinel lymph node is identified, removed, and examined to determine whether cancer cells are present. A sentinel lymph node is the first lymph node(s) to which cancer cells are most likely to spread from a primary tumor. A sentinel lymph node biopsy (SLNB) can be used to help determine the extent, or stage, of cancer in the body. A negative SLNB result suggests that cancer has not developed the ability to spread to nearby lymph nodes or other organs. A positive SLNB result indicates that cancer is present in the sentinel lymph node and may be present in other nearby lymph nodes (called regional lymph nodes) and, possibly, other organs. This information can help a doctor determine the stage of the cancer (extent of the disease within the body) and develop an appropriate treatment plan. (Reference: National Cancer Institute; http://www.cancer.gov/cancertopics/factsheet/detection/sentinel-node-biopsy)
8. CTs: Computed tomography (CT) is a diagnostic procedure that uses special x-ray equipment to obtain cross-sectional pictures of the body. The CT computer displays these pictures as detailed images of organs, bones, and other tissues. (Reference: National Cancer Institute; http://www.cancer.gov/cancertopics/factsheet/detection/CT)
9. MRIs: Magnetic resonance imaging (MRI) is a procedure in which radio waves and a powerful magnet linked to a computer are used to create detailed pictures of areas inside the body. These pictures can show the difference between normal and diseased tissue. MRI makes better images of organs and soft tissue than other scanning techniques, such as computed tomography (CT) or x-ray. MRI is especially useful for imaging the brain, the spine, the soft tissue of joints, and the inside of bones. (Reference: National Cancer Institute; http://www.cancer.gov/dictionary?cdrid=45788)
10. BRCA Gene mutation test: BRCA1 and BRCA2 are human genes that belong to a class of genes known as tumor suppressors. A woman's lifetime risk of developing breast and/or ovarian cancer is greatly increased if she inherits a

NOTES

harmful mutation in *BRCA1* or *BRCA2*. Such a woman has an increased risk of developing breast and/or ovarian cancer at an early age. Genetic counseling before and after a BRCA test is very important to help the patient understand the benefits and the risks of a positive outcome. (Reference: National Cancer Institute; http://www.cancer.gov/cancertopics/factsheet/Risk/BRCA)

The Surgeries
1. Tissue expanders: Breast reconstruction surgery can be either immediate or delayed. In a delayed reconstruction a tissue expander is placed under the skin during the mastectomy to preserve space for an implant while the tissue that was removed is examined. These implants can be inserted underneath the skin and chest muscle that remain after a mastectomy, usually as part of a two-stage procedure. In the first stage, the surgeon places a device called an expander under the chest muscle. The expander is slowly filled with saline during visits to the doctor after surgery. In the second stage, after the chest tissue has relaxed and healed enough, the expander is removed and replaced with an implant. If the surgical team decides that the woman does not need radiation therapy, an implant can be placed where the tissue expander was without further delay. However, if the woman will need to have radiation therapy after mastectomy, her breast reconstruction can be delayed until after radiation therapy is complete. (Reference: National Cancer Institute; http://www.cancer.gov/cancertopics/factsheet/Therapy/breast-reconstruction)

Chemo Starts
1. Chemoterapy: Chemotherapy (also called chemo) is a type of cancer treatment that uses drugs to destroy cancer cells. Chemotherapy works by stopping or slowing the growth of cancer cells, which grow and divide quickly. But it can also harm healthy cells that divide quickly, such as those that line your mouth and intestines or cause your hair to grow. Damage to healthy cells may cause side effects. Often, side effects get better or go away after chemotherapy is over. The choice of chemotherapy depends on the cancer you have. (Reference: National Cancer Institute; http://www.cancer.gov/cancertopics/coping/chemotherapy-and-you/page2)
2. Clegg, H., y Miletello, G. (2006). *Eating Well Through Cancer: Easy Recipes & Recommendations During & After Treatment*. Nashville: Favorite Recipes Press.
3. Spurgeon, C. H. *Morning and Evening: Daily Readings.* Grand Rapids, MI: Christian Classics Ethereal Library.

A Source of Inspiration

NOTES

1. Oram, H., and Kitamura, S. (1992). *A Boy Wants a Dinosaur*. Red Fox Picture Books.

Coping with Neutropenia
1. Peripheral neuropathy - A nerve problem that causes pain, numbness, tingling, swelling, or muscle weakness in different parts of the body. It usually begins in the hands or feet and gets worse over time. Peripheral neuropathy may be caused by physical injury, infection, toxic substances, disease (such as cancer, diabetes, kidney failure, or malnutrition), or drugs, including anticancer drugs. [Reference: National Cancer Institute; http://www.cancer.gov/dictionary?CdrID=44705]

Coping with Uncertainty
1. Adjuvant therapy: Additional cancer treatment given after the primary treatment to lower the risk that the cancer will come back. Adjuvant therapy may include chemotherapy, radiation therapy, hormone therapy, targeted therapy, or biological therapy. (Reference: National Cancer Institute; http://www.cancer.gov/dictionary?cdrid=45587)
Adjuvant therapy for breast cancer is any treatment given after primary therapy to increase the chance of long-term survival. Patients who have a higher risk of breast cancer recurrence are more likely to need adjuvant therapy. Doctors look at both prognostic and predictive factors to decide which patients might benefit from adjuvant treatments. Even in early-stage breast cancer, cells may break away from the primary tumor and spread to other parts of the body. Therefore, doctors give adjuvant therapy to kill any cancer cells that may have spread, even if these cannot be detected by imaging or laboratory tests. (Reference: National Cancer Institute; http://www.cancer.gov/cancertopics/factsheet/Therapy/adjuvant-breast)

Coping with Appearance
1. Tissue expanders: In a delayed reconstruction a tissue expander is placed under the skin during the mastectomy to preserve space for an implant while the tissue that was removed is examined. These implants can be inserted underneath the skin and chest muscle that remain after a mastectomy, usually as part of a two-stage procedure. In the first stage, the surgeon places a device called an expander under the chest muscle. The expander is slowly filled with saline during visits to the doctor after surgery. In the second stage, after the chest tissue has relaxed and healed enough, the expander is removed and replaced with an implant. If the surgical team decides that the woman does not need radiation therapy, an implant can be placed where the tissue expander was without further delay. However, if the woman will need to have radiation therapy after mastectomy, her breast

NOTES

reconstruction can be delayed until after radiation therapy is complete. (Reference: National Cancer Institute; http://www.cancer.gov/cancertopics/factsheet/Therapy/breast-reconstruction)

Coping with the "Leftovers"
1. Chemo Brain: For years cancer survivors have worried about, joked about, and been frustrated by the mental cloudiness they sometimes notice before, during, and after cancer treatment. Even though its exact cause isn't always known, this mental fog is commonly called chemo brain. Patients have been aware of chemo brain for some time, but only recently have studies been done that could help to explain it. Doctors have known for years that radiation treatment to the brain can cause thinking and memory problems. Recently, they have found that chemo is linked to some of the same kinds of problems. Research shows that some cancer drugs can cause certain kinds of changes in the brain. But it also shows that chemo and radiation aren't the only things that can cause thinking and memory problems in people with cancer. Though the brain usually recovers over time, the sometimes vague yet distressing mental changes cancer patients notice are real, not imagined. They might last a short time, or they might go on for years. These changes can make people unable to go back to their school, work, or social activities, or make it so that it takes a lot of mental effort to do so. Chemo brain changes affect everyday life for many people, and more research is needed to help prevent and cope with them.
(Referencia: American Cancer Society; http://www.cancer.org/treatment/treatmentsandsideeffects/physicalsideeffects/chemotherapyeffects/chemo-brain)
2. Lymphedema: Lymphedema is the build-up of fluid in soft body tissues when the lymph system is damaged or blocked. Occurs when the lymph system is damaged or blocked. Fluid builds up in soft body tissues and causes swelling. It is a common problem that may be caused by cancer and cancer treatment. Lymphedema usually affects an arm or leg. The lymph system may be damaged or blocked by infection, injury, cancer, removal of lymph nodes, radiation to the affected area, or scar tissue from radiation therapy or surgery.
(Reference: National Cancer Institute; http://www.cancer.gov/cancertopics/pdq/supportivecare/lymphedema/Patient/page1)

A New Song
1. Psalms 40, NLT:
    [1] I waited patiently for the Lord to help me, and he turned to me and heard my cry.

NOTES

² He lifted me out of the pit of despair, out of the mud and the mire. He set my feet on solid ground and steadied me as I walked along.

³ He has given me a new song to sing, a hymn of praise to our God.
Many will see what he has done and be amazed. They will put their trust in the Lord.

⁴ Oh, the joys of those who trust the Lord, who have no confidence in the proud or in those who worship idols.

⁵ O Lord my God, you have performed many wonders for us. Your plans for us are too numerous to list. You have no equal. If I tried to recite all your wonderful deeds, I would never come to the end of them.

⁶ You take no delight in sacrifices or offerings. Now that you have made me listen, I finally understand—you don't require burnt offerings or sin offerings.

⁷ Then I said, "Look, I have come. As is written about me in the Scriptures:

⁸ I take joy in doing your will, my God, for your instructions are written on my heart."

⁹ I have told all your people about your justice. I have not been afraid to speak out, as you, O Lord, well know.

¹⁰ I have not kept the good news of your justice hidden in my heart; I have talked about your faithfulness and saving power. I have told everyone in the great assembly of your unfailing love and faithfulness.

¹¹ Lord, don't hold back your tender mercies from me. Let your unfailing love and faithfulness always protect me.

¹² For troubles surround me—too many to count! My sins pile up so high I can't see my way out. They outnumber the hairs on my head. I have lost all courage.

¹³ Please, Lord, rescue me! Come quickly, Lord, and help me.

¹⁴ May those who try to destroy me be humiliated and put to shame. May those who take delight in my trouble be turned back in disgrace.

¹⁵ Let them be horrified by their shame, for they said, "Aha! We've got him now!"

¹⁶ But may all who search for you be filled with joy and gladness in you. May those who love your salvation repeatedly shout, "The Lord is great!"

¹⁷ As for me, since I am poor and needy, let the Lord keep me in his thoughts. You are my helper and my savior. O my God, do not delay.

www.ingramcontent.com/pod-product-compliance
Lightning Source LLC
Chambersburg PA
CBHW022356040426
42450CB00005B/212